What do I have to do - break my neck?

What do I have to do - break my neck?

ERLING AND MARGE WOLD

AUGSBURG PUBLISHING HOUSE
Minneapolis, Minnesota

WHAT DO I HAVE TO DO, BREAK MY NECK?

Copyright © 1974 Augsburg Publishing House

Library of Congress Catalog Card No. 73-88604

International Standard Book No. 0-8066-1407-2

Scripture quotations unless otherwise noted are from the Revised Standard Version, copyright 1946 and 1952 by the Division of Christian Education of the National Council of Churches, and are used by permission. Scripture quotations from the Living Bible (LB), copyright 1971 by Tyndale House Publishers, are used by permission.

MANUFACTURED IN THE UNITED STATES OF AMERICA

What do I have to do -- break my neck?

1. To Experience Death and Resurrection   7

2. To Discover the Family of God   17

3. To Wrestle with the Meaning of Suffering   27

4. To Become Aware of My Own Family   42

5. To Drain Power from the Promises of God   58

6. To Explore the Dimensions of Prayer   68

7. To Experience an Invasion of Pure Grace   77

8. To Be Lifted by Hope   92

9. To Come Alive as a Witness   103

    Epilog   111

1 to experience death and resurrection

WHAT DO I HAVE TO DO - - BREAK MY NECK?

My journey into grace began on an unforgettable sunlit summer afternoon. Nothing in nature has lured me more seductively than the ocean. We spent as much vacation time as we could near the waters of the Pacific, walking its beaches, body surfing its waves, and studying its marine fascinations.

On that August day, its dancing, shimmering beauty was at its irresistible best. I yielded to its tug as I ran into the breakers, shivering as they broke about me, but warmed inside by their exploding gaiety. I hadn't planned to stay in long, wanting only to ride a couple of waves to shore. Little did I realize that this was to be the last time I would ever give my body to that mighty surf!

As I surfaced from a dive, shaking my head to get the water out of my eyes, I looked up just in time to see the largest wave that I had ever seen in a dozen summers of surfing. My choices were clear: dive into it, or turn to swim with it. That second of hesitation was costly, and the huge breaker bore down on me with such speed that I couldn't even turn before it hit. Catching me off balance, it struck me broadside with all the force of its immense weight. In the crushing turbulence of that wall of water, my body twisted as helplessly as a piece of driftwood. My head smashed hard against the ocean floor, the force of the blow momentarily stunning me.

Consciousness brought with it the awareness that I was floating face down on the swelling surface of the Pacific, knowing only a vast numbness of body and limbs and the bitter taste of salt water in my nose and mouth. My tongue pushed forward against the jagged edges of broken teeth. My head and my hands were hanging down. Total paralysis gripped me, and I knew that my muscles no longer responded to my will. Knowledge of my predicament was instantaneous; I was completely at the mercy of the sea, suspended helplessly at the very edge of death.

Body surfing is an exciting sport. If you catch a wave right before it breaks, it carries your body like a human surfboard—arms stretched above your head, body taut, feet pointing — in a wildly exhilarating ride straight down to the beach! After several such engagements with the waves, one leaves the ocean exhausted but renewed. Besides the physical renewal, part of the fascination of body surfing undoubtedly lies in the dangers inherent in challenging the mighty Pacific to share its powers with pygmy humans.

Erling would often go down alone to the ocean, and if I questioned the wisdom of this, he usually responded in the same way all of us have done when we want to discount the dangers in doing something we love: "What

8

could happen? And besides, there are always other people on the beach, and someone would notice if anything went wrong."

But on that particular day we went down together, and I sat on the beach with a friend who had come from northern California for a visit and who was not prepared to swim. The sun dropped its rays on the bright beach and scattered them on the sea. We talked, lulled into relaxation by the warmth of the sand and the roar of the surf, trusting that those tiny dark figures down in the water were watching out for each other.

The scimitar-shaped stretch of beach between Abalone Point and Scotchman's Cove is one of the loveliest spots in the southern California coastline. Its moods vary from fog-shrouded gray to the multi-colored intoxication of clear salty air blown between blue sky and sea. Lying just north of Laguna Beach, it bursts suddenly into view as the coast highway comes over the hill at El Morro Canyon. It's a bit of God's creation that never fails to trigger a celebrative response to its beauty.

I wiggled my toes in the sand as my attention wandered from one distraction to another—the cry of seagulls overhead, a bright orange sail on the horizon, the spray of breakers striking the Point. A little signal broke in my consciousness when I noticed that the breakers were hitting with unusual force that day. Perhaps it's getting too rough for the children, I thought.

Suddenly alert to the dangers of a heavy surf, I sat up and began checking the water. Paul, Erling's assistant pastor was there; our son Erling was near him; Paul's younger sister was in the shallows with our granddaughter Kimmie; but where were my husband and daughter Kristi?

Kristi reappeared from a wave and pushed her long blond hair from her eyes and face. Still no Erling. Kristi

9

looked around, following the procedures of our informal "buddy" system. She disappeared behind a wave, and when she again became visible, I realized that Paul and young Erling were hurrying toward her in water-bound slow motion. Erling was nowhere in sight.

"I think something's happened to Erling," I said to Carol, as I ran down the beach and plunged, clothed in slacks and shirt, into the foaming waters.

I have never been more consciously alive. Time was held captive to the moment. My mind, sensitized to my situation, raced around the possibilities open to me. Ignoring the sting of the salt water, my eyes were caught and held by an ethereal light to my right—a light which illuminated the waters to their depth before sweeping out into the sea.

In that moment, I knew the presence of the one to whom I had long since given my life, Jesus Christ.

My glad heart heard the words of David and echoed them, "I keep the Lord always before me; because he is at my right hand, I shall not be moved" (Ps. 16:8).

Imagine how my heart leaped at the wonder of the fact that he was really there in the water with me and that this might be the time when he would say to me, "Come on over to my side. The party is about to begin, and I'll show you what I'll do for the one whom I delight to honor." That's what the light appeared to hold in its core—the possibility of an endless surprise party. Ecstasy grabbed me with the vision of that inviting presence, and I knew the wonder of St. Paul's chief desire: "That I may know him and the power of his resurrection." Physical death and resurrection loomed as valid options for me, and I yearned to go to him in total joy.

The glory of the light warmed me with a sense of freedom and complete personal abandon. All of the emotions inside of me welled up to cry, "If this is my moment I'll be thrilled to come, my Lord! I've waited my lifetime for this. Release me and take me with you forever!"

This prayer of relinquishment brought such peace that the salt in my eyes became tears of uncontrollable joy.

With the peace two new convictions gripped me.

I was paralyzed! I tried to swim toward the light, but I couldn't move. There was no way I could get to that inviting Presence. He was beyond my reach, a promise not to be realized.

A confession, born of my helplessness, took shape. "I know that I'm paralyzed, Lord. I can't move at all. Something's wrong with my body. If you want me to remain this way, I accept it with joy from your hands."

A flash glimpse of the implications of my helpless condition became visual reality: long hospitalization, a permanent wheelchair, total helplessness. But, in the timeless confrontation of the moment, I accepted them all with willing abandon, secure in the presence to my right.

The other conviction became a clear longing. I saw my wife, my children, my grandchildren, my parishioners, and some of the friends I loved. How much I suddenly longed to continue to share life with them, and especially in this whole new dimension of Christ's reality! I even thought of a family without a father, and an income cut off, of restrictive life-changes, of a lack of educational opportunities for the younger children.

I had no sooner accepted all of these possibilities as viable alternatives from the hand of God, when I realized that someone was turning my body over in the water. I looked up into the terror-stricken face of my daughter Kristi. Her hair swept across my face as she cried, "Dad, are you all right?"

The current swept me out of her grasp. Blackness descended, then once more I felt the tug of her arms pulling me back from the clutching sea.

Only one intense desire consumed me at this moment: I knew I had to get out of the water. Summoning all the power I could manage, I whispered to Kristi, "Call Mom."

Her frantic screams brought help. I felt other hands holding me firmly, and when I saw Marge, I was glad and knew everything would be all right. In moments I was stretched on the beach just beyond the reach of the hungry waves. Wet sand was packed around my neck, and I was happy someone thought of shading me with a beach umbrella since I sunburn so easily. I heard excited talk about calling an ambulance.

My breath came with difficulty and Marge asked, "Do you want one of us to give you mouth-to-mouth?"

My eyes must have revealed my need, because Paul leaned over and breathed into me. I felt his soft beard against my face and felt Marge pinching my nose shut as air filled my lungs.

Hundreds of times in my ministry I had watched people struggle for breath as death approached. Death had never been merely an academic subject for me, but a mysterious reality whose secrets I longed to probe. My childhood home adjoined the church, and I often heard its bell toll three-times-three whenever a funeral cortege left its sanctuary for the last mile-long journey to the village graveyard.

With great clarity, I recalled a death encounter in my childhood. I was thrown into a swimming hole at the bend of a river by an older friend who didn't know I was unable to swim. I went down for the third time before he pulled me out. During those moments of drowning my mind came strangely alive, and everything I had ever said or done came into clear focus. My mind became a projection chamber where a thousand films were shown simultaneously, a vivid review of my brief life history. Nothing was hidden from me, let alone from the God with whom we all have to do. Caught up by that unforgettable experience, I had never questioned St. Paul's preview of a judgment day in Romans 14:12, "Each of us shall give account of himself to God."

Lying on the beach, I was filled with an intensity of joy, for the intervening years had taught me the wonder of Romans 8:1, "There is therefore now no condemnation for those who are in Christ Jesus."

In the water I had met death, and this encounter with the Grim Reaper had illuminated that conviction! Death has no sting! Life for a Christian is a reality on both sides!

With the breaking of the light at my right side, Life possessed me. Jesus was "for real" when he promised, "I am the resurrection and the life. He that lives and believes in me shall never die." Life is a continuity to anyone who is alive to his promise.

I remember so many who have made peace with their own death through faith in Jesus.

I remember Charlie in Texas. The light came on in his soul one Sunday afternoon as the slanting sun struggled to illumine the room in which a small group of us were talking about the resurrection. Charlie had fought a long fight with the despairs of alcoholism and now he had lung cancer. He appeared awed when he left the room that afternoon, saying with a bold, new assurance, "Now I'm beginning to see." That week he gently marked with a colored pen all of the promises in the Gospels which he was "seeing," such as, "Come unto me, all ye who labor and are heavy laden, and I will give you rest" (Matt. 11:28 kjv). Fulfillment followed promise when death came peacefully to Charlie only a week later.

I remember Norma. She came to a hospital in our community as a terminal cancer patient. A large inoperable tumor prohibited her from swallowing, but not from smiling in the face of death. Her hospital room glowed with the presence of Life. An exuberance poured from her spirit and filled her room. No one needed to ask, "Do you have to wait to die before you really experience resurrection?" Her person was radiant with the Lord of Life, who makes it clear that we can have his life whenever we want it—now!

Life and death as opposite sides of the same reality are to be lived fully. We are here to feel, to explore, to encounter, to know. Dying is a part of our life experience. To never reckon with its reality is to be in "lifelong bondage" through the fear of death (Heb. 2:15).

On the edge of death, the promise of life is as real as was the distant wail of the siren singing its message of rescue and hope to those of us who waited on the beach. As the volume of sound became an unbearable scream, there was a flurry of movement in the group of people hovering over me.

"His lips are turning blue," I heard someone say. Behind me, someone else was sobbing.

I was beginning to feel a need for more air in my lungs and desperately fought a rising nausea.

Somewhere close by, the siren died, swallowed up by the pounding surf. Car doors slammed and I sensed rather than heard the dull tympani of feet running on wet sand.

The ambulance had arrived, just in time.

This can't be me riding in an ambulance down the middle of the main street of Laguna Beach, I thought.

14

That man in the back, lying so still, body so pale and sand-covered, an oxygen mask strapped to his face—that can't be my husband. Things like this don't happen to people like us, only to the people you read about in the newspapers.

I stole a glance at the driver. He was preoccupied with guiding the ambulance through the bumper-to-bumper resort traffic, steering skillfully between the cars scurrying out of our way. With his right hand he manipulated a switch which changed the configuration of sounds coming from the siren above us. I noted with detachment that the siren sounded much farther away than I thought it would when sitting right underneath it.

With the same curious disinterest, I was aware of the stares of the people on the sidewalks, wondering as I had often wondered about people in hurrying ambulances. Their unspoken question was the same as mine: Was the man back there dead or alive?

I turned around and looked. Another ambulance attendant and one of the life guards were with Erling. One held the collar around his neck, the other was checking his pulse and blood pressure.

Erling's eyes were closed and his chest was quiet. I learned later that all of the intercostal muscles were paralyzed, those muscles that make us able to expand the chest voluntarily in order to breathe more deeply. The only thing that kept him breathing was the involuntary movement of the diaphragm, but it wasn't enough to supply his body with all of its need for oxygen.

I should be crying. I had had to speak very firmly to Kristi before the ambulance left, telling her to be happy she had saved her father's life and reminding her that she would have to take care of the younger children and our guests while I went to the hospital. At least it had checked her hysteria and given her something concrete to think about and to do.

The driver radioed a terse, coded message to someone in a hospital somewhere telling them we were coming in. I shivered, conscious of the wet clothes clinging coldly to my body. Sand ground into my skin and irritated the soles of my feet. Well, I'm feeling, so that means that I can't be dreaming, anyway. Who said, "I feel therefore I am"?

What dumb things to be thinking at a time like this, I thought. I should be praying, "God, help Erling!" At that moment, blocking out every stray thought, every transient feeling, came the answer that was to sustain me and flood me with enduring joy through all the months that followed that day, "This illness is not unto death; it is for the glory of God, so that the Son of God may be glorified by means of it" (John 11:4).

I believe you, God! Now tears pricked my eyes. God was with us! Erling was alive, and no matter what happened, we were in God's hands! A surge of love for my Lord and for my husband suffused me and I praised God!

The long journey was over. We had arrived at the hospital.

2 | to discover the family of god

Paralyzed! The word nagged at the corners of my mind as sensory tests were administered in the hospital. I don't remember how many people scratched the soles of my feet, pricked my skin in various places, and asked over and over again, "Do you feel that? Let me see if you can wiggle your toes. Can you lift your finger?"

Except for some slight movement of my toes, the answer was always negative. The slightest touch anywhere on my body brought a shuddering tingle everywhere at once, a phenomenon totally beyond my control. While I felt no normal sensation, the sand on my body was magnified into the sharpness of a million needles by some strange magnification of sensitivity resulting from my spinal cord injury.

How many times I had preached on the Bible text, "Four men arrived carrying a paralyzed man on a stretcher. They couldn't get to Jesus through the crowd, so they dug through the clay roof above his head and

17

lowered the sick man on his stretcher, right down in front of Jesus" (Mark 2:34 LB).

Now *I* was the paralyzed man. There was no way whatsoever that I could move or help myself. I could *will* to move, but my muscles refused to obey my will.

I lay on the stretcher in the Emergency Room. My nose, eyes, and ears itched unbearably from the dried salt water, but my hands would not respond to the need to scratch myself or brush the salt away. The sand under the elastic swimming trunks ground like broken glass into my waist, but I couldn't shift my position to relieve the pressure.

Doctors worked over me. A tube was put down into my stomach through my nose to relieve the threatening nausea. Holes were drilled into the sides of my head so that metal tongs could be inserted into my skull and weights suspended from them. X-rays were taken, and three fractured vertebrae in my neck were discovered.

In this frantic sea of human activity, of comings and goings, of sharply enunciated orders and intercom pagings, only *I* was immobile. Though fully conscious and completely aware, without those trained and caring hands working over me, I was a dead man!

Gradually, the spotlight of the Spirit was to shift its focus for me in the Gospel account of the paralyzed man. Naturally, I could never again forget that the drama of my life had been abruptly rewritten to cast me in the lead role of the paralytic. But while the marvel of that man's healing and walking had always been the highlight of the story before, throughout my paralysis my attention was caught instead by those four caring persons who stopped at nothing to bring help to the helpless one.

I had discovered the absolute importance of the caring family of God!

The Emergency Room receptionist went down the list of items on the form in her typewriter. "Name? Address? Age?" I answered automatically, conscious of my disheveled appearance and wet sandy clothes in that antiseptic environment.

The lifeguard who had ridden in the back of the ambulance with Erling came out of the Emergency Room and stopped where I sat.

"Don't worry about your husband," he consoled me. "I fell off my board about a month ago and they brought me in here. You wait, he'll be out of here in no time, as healthy as I am."

I saw his strong tanned body topped by a shock of sun-bleached hair, and smiled. His worried blue eyes betrayed his attempt to be reassuring.

"Thank you," I said, "I'm sure he'll be all right."

I turned back to the receptionist, ready to apologize for the interruption to her information-gathering, when I noticed the tears in her eyes.

"I'm sorry," she said, dabbing at her eyes with a white tissue. "I shouldn't be acting this way, but your husband's the third person brought in in two weeks who's broken his neck in a surfing accident. Forgive me, but I just can't help feeling bad about it."

She cares, I thought, she really cares. And so does the young lifeguard.

I no longer felt quite so alone in that alien place. Erling was in the hands of people who cared.

The church is called to be a caring community. That's God's dream for his own family. There's almost a desperation in his passion to make of it a caring and a carrying community of love. The caring comes out of an act of the heart, but it must be fused to the action imposed

19

by Jesus to "bear one another's burden." Only then can we fulfill the will of God.

Neither the caring nor the carrying can ever be alone. The test of the word is the work.

I discovered that Jesus Christ sees beyond the facade, the outer form, the inhibiting masks, to the person. He has no hang-ups when it comes to race or background; he overlooks completely all individual idiosyncrasies. All he's concerned with is the wholeness of persons.

I caught a glimpse of this caring community in the hospital's Intensive Care Unit. The story of the four friends of the paralytic came to life. They were there in the persons of the hospital staff, the doctors, the nurses, the therapists, the cleaning women, the electricians, the technicians. They were united in a common purpose, to bring wholeness to each patient.

What's the point of the whole Christian church but this?

I was fascinated one night to see the concentration on one man's need. All day I had been aware of a new patient brought into the adjoining coronary care unit. The conversations of the nurses indicated how desperately ill he was. In the middle of the night there was a sudden commotion in his direction. Out of the corner of my eye, I saw with horror that he had leaped in delirium from his bed falling flat on the floor and pulling out the oxygen tube, the wires, all the lifelines that were sustaining him.

Even before my scream was out of my mouth, every member of the staff in that room had jumped to his rescue. In seconds they had lifted him (those caring hands again) back into bed as the coronary emergency unit burst into the room with its specialized life-saving equipment. With terrifying urgency, they fought to save one man's life.

Every moment of it intrigued me with its implications for the body of Christ. They wanted total wholeness. Each member of the team knew his or her special gifts in the restoration process. I sensed no fighting for place or tension among them, only a freedom and a joy in the knowledge that each one's contribution was vital to the whole.

My discovery of the sacramental character of the family of God began for me with the hands of Kristi turning me over in the water. I was saved! From that moment on I could only lie there on the beach and in the hospital and watch the grace of God operate through the hands that preserved and restored my life.

There were the anonymous hands that formed a living cradle in which I was carried tenderly out of the water and laid gently high up on the beach. The memory of my young son's hands supporting my neck so very carefully warms my heart. The strong hands of the lifeguard packing my neck with wet sand and the cushioning hands of the ambulance attendant who immobilized my head on that long ride to the hospital. The professional hands of the neurosurgeons who drilled the tongs into my skull, while he quipped, "If you feel anything, I've gone too far."

All of the hands were necessary.

With the coming of the Spirit at Pentecost, all orders, divisions, and hierarchies were lost in "the common good." The Joel prophecy quoted in Acts 2:17-18 states that God poured out his Spirit on "all flesh." Not just on lords and masters, not just on men, not just on the old and the venerable.

The Spirit broke down all the ancient barriers! All the spiritual gifts and fruits were given to all without discrimination: sons and daughters, the young as well as the old, the slaves, both men and women. Economic status was dismissed as unimportant because "all who believed were together and had all things in common" (Acts 2:44).

All persons in the family of God were of equal importance and each one's gifts were necessary. "Now there are varieties of service, but the same Lord; and there are varieties of working, but it is the same God who inspires them all in every one. To each is given the manifestation of the Spirit for the common good" (1 Cor. 12:4-7).

Men place economic and ecclesiastical price tags on the gifts God gives. As far as God is concerned there are no degrees of importance in his family. There is only the Spirit and his gifts, and they are to be used to speak to the needs of each member of the family.

All of the hands were necessary, but some stand out with more clarity in the kaleidoscope of events. Genuine love flowed from Ray, the nurse who had served as a medic in Vietnam, encircling everyone his life touched. Even the warm German accent of Clara, the older nurse, was comforting. She could have quit nursing since her husband was employed, but, as she told me, "Sometimes I think I should go on half time, but when I see all this suffering and know how hard it is to get trained help in ICU, I stay." Then, with gentle pathos, she added, "What else can I do?"

Bill was a weightlifter, some 265 pounds strong. As the troubleshooter, he was always called for the more difficult assignments. Bill had become a nurse because as a sixteen-year-old he had spent eight months in a body cast. A speeding motorist had hit him while he was cycling.

"I wasn't very nice to the nurses," he told me. "I was hospitalized 18 months and all my pain made me impossible to get along with. But they were still so kind to me that I guess it sort of broke my heart. When I finished high school, I took nurses' training because it seemed the best way to say thank you for what they'd done for me."

I, who had never been hospitalized before, marveled at the love with which the hospital attendants performed even the most unpleasant tasks. All those functions of the body which good health takes for granted stopped when I broke my neck. They had to be performed for me by other people's hands. I became convinced that no one could do some of those jobs even to earn a salary. Only a profound concern for other human beings could motivate people to serve this way.

I had seen some of this caring love manifested in the church, but there were times when I saw the servant Lord very clearly in the hospital even in the service of those who did not otherwise acknowledge his lordship in their lives. And then I knew that all people are God's people because they are made in his image, and that image cannot help but reveal itself in all loving vocation.

And then there was the family that lived outside the Intensive Care Unit. In a corner of the hall stood half a dozen straightbacked chairs upholstered in dull orange plastic. That corner served as a waiting room for relatives of the critically ill persons inside. For one month that corner was my sanctuary.

A building program had been in progress at the hospital for a year, and the wall facing us at the end of the corridor was covered with colored metal rectangles with names printed on them. I stared at them for hours. Mrs. A., Alex's Grocery, The Peterson Co., L.'s Realty, Dr. and Mrs. Edward S. No other explanation. Maybe, I thought, they had given money for the new wing. Maybe they had died in that corner, and a wry humor tugged at me with the thought of another rectangle up there labeled, Mrs. Erling Wold. I want mine colored orange. I never asked anyone about them, but I spent an infinity of unseeing moments studying those meaningless bits of metal.

Although normally an avid reader, I never read one word while I sat there. Only one thing focused my attention, the door to my left. All that mattered was that door —who went in, who came out, the sounds, the screams, and getting inside four times a day at 8:30, 12:30, 5:30 and 8 o'clock, for ten minutes at a time.

The rest of the time we waited—all of us who were united by our ties to those sheet-covered persons in the room behind the closed door, all of them victims of the surf.

There was Jim, 18 years old, whose surfboard had been flipped by a wave, hurling him headfirst into the sand. He had just been voted "Class Clown" or some such title at his high school graduation, so his friends thought he was kidding when he rolled around in the surf asking for help. His neck was broken and he was paralyzed.

There was Stan, 25 years old. Stan was the carefree hippie who loved the ocean and the excitement of body surfing. He was out alone when a wave caught him. Because he was alone it was some time before a nearby swimmer realized that he was in trouble and came to pull him out. Stan's spine was the most severely damaged of all and he was unable to undergo surgery until a week after his accident because of the instability of his blood pressure.

Josh was only 12 years old. He and his brother were playing in the surf when a wave rolled onto the beach, picked him up and dashed him down, breaking his neck. His eight-year-old brother thought he was just rolling in the water, and his father had just gone to get some hot

24

dogs. Other swimmers realized that the boy was hurt and picked him up out of the water. Josh was not completely paralyzed.

Jim's folks drove a distance of forty miles one way every day to see him for at least three of those four ten-minute visiting periods. This meant making arrangements for five other children, two slightly older than Jim, three younger. They were Catholic.

Stan's folks had been summoned from the Midwest by his girl friend, and they came every day from their motel room to sit outside the ICU door for 10 to 12 hours a day. Stan's dad was a Baptist lay preacher and a teacher in a school for the handicapped.

Joshua's folks were devout Mormons, and Josh had already been ordained a deacon in his church. His dad had taken Josh and his brother with him from Utah to Laguna to share a weekend business trip. His mother flew down the day of Josh's surgery.

For two months these people were my support group in that waiting room. We shared our prayers, our faith, and those worn plastic chairs.

Describing that waiting room fellowship, Josh's dad said to the rest of us, "I can't believe this group of people! The only way I describe what exists between all of us is by comparing it to Christmas. At that time, everyone is your friend, and you all feel you have something in common because of that baby born in Bethlehem."

Jesus was our great common denominator, and we knew that even though outside of that hospital there were structures and relationships that would divide us, nevertheless we were one in our common need for each other and for the strength that had to be found in God's grace as it was ministered through our fellowship.

Each of us had our days of crisis, days when a sudden turn for the worse gripped one of the patients, days of *agonizing through long five-to-eight-hour surgeries, days of bladder infections or pneumonia and high fevers or erratic blood pressure. On these days the affected family was encircled by the others, praying, touching, comforting, sharing. Frequently we gathered at the end of the day for an impromptu time of prayer in the deserted parking ramp. A cup of coffee in the basement cafeteria became a supportive encounter when hopes and fears could be shared.*

"Jim picked up his own toast at breakfast this morning," his father beamingly informed us after one visiting time. That announcement occasioned a mild celebration. After all, if Jim had some return of function, that sparked hope in the rest of us.

And hope was something we all lived on.

Marge told me about the fellowship of prayer that supported us—thousands of cards and letters from friends and strangers all over the world, an outpouring of love and support that made me weep even as I praised God for his family. How could anyone deny that grace was the sacramental gift of the community of believers? The amazing riches of the fellowship overwhelmed us.

But why does it take tragedy, disaster, and hardship to pull together our lonely islands of being?

3 to wrestle with the meaning of suffering

I had never known physical pain before my accident. My only encounters with suffering came through countless pastoral visits in hospitals and in the homes of those who were undergoing physical agonies. Sometimes one absorbs another person's pain through involvement in the other's suffering. Anyone who cares suffers vicariously.

For instance, I remember my contacts with Jim. He was arrested in our town and convicted of the strangulation murder of two young women. The police called me at midnight when he was taken into custody. Through the months of his internment and trial, I agonized with him in his solitary prison cell. In that cheerless, windowless rectangle of steel and concrete, I experienced the same torments of confinement and the same hopeless despair as he when he was finally sentenced to two terms of life imprisonment.

Just as bitter is the identification with the psychic problems of people: the despair of those whom life has trapped in some hopeless corner; the loneliness of those who feel unloved and unwanted; the depression of men and women abandoned by their mates. I was often brought to the edge of exhaustion by entering into the psychological difficulties of others.

But these were vicarious sufferings, and the possibility always exists of escaping from the trials of other people. I could walk out of Jim's cell through the three locked prison doors that separated him from the world outside into my own freedom. When my visits were completed, I could escape from the psychiatric wards and the medical and surgical halls of the hospital into the wholeness of life outside. I often gloried afterwards in my own good health.

And then came August 10th. Now *I* was the sufferer, imprisoned on the narrow Stryker frame, impaled by tongs in my skull to sandbag weights dangling behind my bed. Pain gripped my head and neck. Later the physical therapy sessions brutally tortured my atrophied muscles, and the convulsive shudderings that followed could be controlled only by drugs.

Why suffering? I wondered through sleepless nights. And this was the aching cry that echoed through every hospital corridor. I heard the groans of an old woman down the hall, the lonely sound of her sufferings breaking through closed doors. I listened to the story of the woman next door who came to see me when I left Intensive Care. She had suffered through tuberculosis, many surgeries, and now was terrorized by the threat of terminal cancer. The man in the bed next to me had been hospitalized 56 days and had had 12 surgeries for bowel obstructions. A brilliant computer specialist — young, wealthy, handsome—suffered constant chest pain and had endured three severe heart attacks. A mother and a father joined sobs in the hall when they witnessed the sufferings of their three-year-old daughter.

How does one resolve the dilemma of suffering?

Even the Bible leaves us to wrestle with this predicament. On the one hand there's the story of Job who is depicted as a righteous and godly man, the victim of excruciating disasters, demanding to know why. The Bible makes it clear that God lets Satan move even into the life of the faithful; and can anyone forget the burning words of Jesus to Peter, "Simon, Simon, behold, Satan demanded to have you, that he might sift you like wheat" (Luke 22:31)? In these pictures Satan is the aggressor.

How then does one interpret Lam. 3:15-16 (LB)? "He has filled me with bitterness and given me a cup of deepest sorrows to drink. He has made me eat gravel and broken my teeth; he has rolled me in ashes and dirt." In my case, these words had been literally fulfilled. Was God the aggressor who had moved against me? But I knew him as a God of love. It's understandable to conceive of Satan as the author and initiator of suffering, but not a loving God.

In California, our home for many years was on the wrong side of the San Andreas fault, and in my suffering I was struck by the realization that there is a great fault running through the wholeness that God planned for his creation. Television specials and magazine articles have made the world aware that the great San Andreas fault —that great rift in the earth which runs the length of the state of California—places the entire coastal area in constant jeopardy. None of us who live there need to be told by the prophets of doom that some day we might tumble into the sea. We have been awakened by the earth's mighty shakings, jigglings, and rollings. Abysses have opened up in roadways ahead and mountains have been lifted and shaken.

Paul paints in vivid imagery the fear-inspiring fact that a great rift runs right through all of existence. We're fighting not against flesh and blood, he says, but against fiendish powers of evil let loose from the headquarters of the evil one (Eph. 6). Fully aware of this fact our Lord taught us to pray, "Deliver us from *the evil*." An illness and suffering are a sign of "the evil." They magnify the fact of the fault running through creation.

So we acknowledge that there is this foreboding rift in creation and that we live in precarious jeopardy from unleashed powers of evil. But the haunting question still remains, Why does a loving God permit suffering?

Does he cause it? What do these words from Lamentations quoted above mean? And what is Isaiah saying when he quotes God, "I form light and create darkness, I make weal and create woe" (45:7)? Amos also questions, "Does evil befall a city, unless the Lord has done it? (3:6).

We cannot admit that there is a self-existent evil power in the world which came into being independent of God's creation or we are trapped in the oriental dualism which posits that there are equally autonomous and powerful good and evil gods in the universe. God is God and from him all things exist.

What then? Is cosmic evil leashed but straining to be about its destructive work in persons and institutions? Does God merely *allow* it to be unleashed? (Cf. Romans 1 and Job 1.)

Thielicke discusses this dilemma in his book, *Our Heavenly Father,* and speaks to it with these thoughts:

Everything God permits the dark powers to do

must *first pass in review before him.* Everything is examined and censored by his fatherly eye to see whether it will really work "for good with those who love him." Everything must first pass by him, every bomb that may strike me, every shell splinter that may take my dearest away from me, every intrigue or chicanery that men may inflict upon me. . . . It is as if God intercepts these originally evil and disastrous missiles of fate, catches them in his fatherly arms, and sends them in the direction he wants them to go for the benefit of his children.

So everything is transformed for those who are his children, for those who have seen the Father in Jesus' life and death, and never again will let him go. Then it comes from his hands; in any case it must go through his hands.

This realization gripped me in my own experience. No matter what happened to me, I was never outside of God's hands. The Presence that I met in the water was with me in my struggle, and he literally carried me. The ecstasy was indefinable. All I know is that when I thought of God, I knew that he was good beyond description.

At night I would awake to weep in sheer gratitude, conscious that his healing presence was intimately mine. I was often embarrassed to ask the nurses to wash the burning tears from my eyes. Only one of them seemed to understand. So few of us seem willing to admit that suffering has any value at all.

Out of the agonies of Auschwitz, Victor Frankl discovered for himself the meaning of suffering: "If there is meaning in life at all, then there must be a meaning in suffering. Suffering is an ineradicable part of life, even as

31

fate and death. Without suffering and death human life cannot be complete." Emerson concluded, "He has seen but half the Universe who never has been shown the house of Pain."

In my sufferings, several "meanings" were significantly mine. It was clear during those months of my hospitalization and convalescence that I had little human value. For all practical purposes I was a "nothing."

If a man's worth is measured by his ability to work and to earn a salary, then I was a "zero." Work requires an output of physical energy, and I could not even move.

If a man's worth is measured by the yardstick of sexual prowess, then my human value was not even measurable, since paralysis had rendered me impotent.

If I had measured my worth by any of these criteria, my suffering would have destroyed me. But the ecstasy that gave wings to my spirit, in spite of my paralysis, was the knowledge that I had immense value with God. He had exchanged his Son for me.

It's one of our cultural hangups to equate infirmity and disability with powerlessness. We are a physical people, dominated by work ethic and materialism. Work and energy produce the means to pay for a proliferation of consumer goods. "Beautiful people" represent the American ideal, and Miss America could never be a victim of cerebral palsy! Can you imagine a magazine center-fold featuring a paralytic?

Then what do we do with St. Paul? He tells us of his constant handicap or infirmity, saying, "Three times I besought the Lord about this, that it should leave me; but he said to me, 'My grace is sufficient for you, for my power is made perfect in weakness.' I will all the more gladly boast of my weaknesses, that the power of Christ may rest upon me. For the sake of Christ, then, I am

32

content with weaknesses, insults, hardships, persecutions, and calamities; for when I am weak, then I am strong" (2 Cor. 12:8-10). And the strength of Paul's testimony is still felt in the lives of individuals centuries removed from him.

The strength of Jesus was never more apparent than when he was hanging helplessly on the cross. The thief on his right was transformed by its impact. The centurion, strong Roman despiser of all things weak, saw God through the helplessness.

Much of this is rhetoric until one experiences it as fact. The strength of the Lord which was revealed in Erling's total disability was a thing of wonder. Nurses expressed amazement; hospital volunteers asked me how this could be; visitors came with comfort and went away renewed and filled. "We came to minister to him," they would say, "and he ministered to us."

The most remarkable testimony came from the Recovery Room nurse. When I was called from the lobby after Erling's five-and-a-half hour surgery, the nurse met me at the door.

"My name is Audrey and I know you're Marge because your husband's been asking for you," she said. "I'm the nurse in charge here, and I want to tell you about the fantastic thing that happened when your husband was brought in from surgery. There was an aura around him that was so powerful that I was overwhelmed by it. I couldn't understand it so I looked at his chart, and when I saw that he was a Lutheran pastor, I knew the reason. I just became a Christian two months ago myself, and I knew that here was a man of God when they brought your husband in."

At the end of that long day Audrey came to sit beside me where I waited and to talk about her life—her divorce, her subsequent search for meaning, and the *strengthening that had now come to her through her experience of God's presence in the Recovery Room that day. She gave me a small book as a gift by which to remember her and asked if her young pastor, who served an independent church, could visit Erling later.*

"So we do not lose heart. Though our outer nature is wasting away, our inner nature is being renewed every day," marvels St. Paul in 2 Cor. 4:16, and I knew that this was empirically true for Erling, if the testimony of those who came in touch with him during his hospitalization can be believed.

It became clear that two choices confronted me. On the one hand I could so easily have surrendered to apathy. The urging question kept nagging at me, *Why struggle, why fight? Why not lie back and let life run its course?* There is an immense appeal to sink into languor; to be hypnotized by one's illness and to be overcome by the vastness of the struggle; to give up and enjoy the irresponsibility of "copping out."

The other choice demands a conscious decision. I willed to be involved in a struggle for wholeness. Everything in me screamed that I would not submit to the pleasantness of torpor. My heart told me that if I had any chance at all of restoration, it lay in never submitting myself to the destructive powers that tried to seduce me into giving up the struggle. I knew that my attitude towards my body in those first days was crucial.

My personal motto had always been rooted in Paul's strong affirmation, "I can do all things through Christ who keeps on pouring his power into me." (Phil. 4:19, in my own literal translation of the Greek.) I grasped at that offered possibility with all of my psychic strength, and the awe and mystery of God's operation within me created an ecstasy that never left me in the nine weeks of my hospitalization. Without question the promises of God gave me a mind-set that helped me picture myself whole. That became my dream and my passion, my second nature. I didn't have to think about doing "my thing," but the power of God grabbed me and propelled me along.

In therapy, any enforced movement was painful. The stretching of joints and ligaments became excruciating. Tears would flow when there was no crying. The therapist, a redemptive disciplinarian, forced me with unremitting fervor. In this setting, a conviction, born of experience, overwhelmed me! Agony with purpose is ecstasy!

From Joe, Erling's therapist, I learned that redemptive love must at times be very tough, even abrasive. I had made the "noble" decision to "dedicate my life" to taking care of Erling if permanent disability was to be his lot. But I soon realized that, if Joe had anything to say about Erling's future, there would be no such self-imposed martyrdom for me!

There was only one possibility for Erling, as far as Joe was concerned. Erling would walk again! In a no-holds-barred, no-quarter-given contest, Joe pitted himself against the enemy which held Erling helplessly bound to his bed. He wrestled with muscles and joints, every day pushing the rebellious tissues beyond their previous limits, ignoring Erling's involuntary tears and groans and the gasping breaths that were short-changed by his crippled chest muscles.

There came the day when Joe decided it was time for his patient to sit up on the edge of the bed. Binding Erling's dangling arms to his body with a towel, Joe told him to get up. Have you ever tried to lift your body from a flat-on-your-back position without the use of your arms and with no ability to raise your legs and get some leverage to hurl your torso up?

I was permitted to watch only after Joe had determined that I would react properly to the procedure. After an agonizing struggle that seemed to go on endlessly, a struggle of floppings and rollings and gruntings, with only occasional suggestions from Joe, Erling was halfway up, only to fall back and be told to try again. An infinite number of tries later, and with a finger's worth of help from Joe, he was finally upright. I was exhausted, but Joe was triumphant!

But not satisfied. Erling's weak muscles were up but not strong enough to keep him up. He began to fall to the right. Joe hit his right arm and bellowed, "I said sit up!" Erling jerked himself upright but began to fall to the left. Joe slapped him on the left arm and bellowed again. Erling's muscles took Joe seriously, and Erling finally sat.

When the day came a few weeks later on which Joe had determined that Erling should stand for the first time, I was again permitted to watch. The same agonizing efforts to pull himself up, without help and with his useless arms bound to his chest, at last resulted in his standing upright.

But his knees buckled. Joe hit Erling's legs, hard, and they jerked themselves straight. They buckled again and again and each time Joe hit them, and said, "I said stand!"

Erling responded to the toughness of Joe's love for him and his ultimate wholeness, and each day Joe pushed him to the limits of his endurance. I know that Erling would still be completely paralyzed had it not been for Joe's "tough love."

To accomplish wholeness, love must sometimes assume this character. Lives are too often crippled because of

36

*the "protection" wrapped around them by the self-serving
needs of solicitous lovers. The need to be needed can
become a selfish monster which devours the independence of others to feed itself.*

*Joe neatly demolished the lovely fantasy cocoon I was
preparing for Erling.*

Suffering must be permitted to do its perfect work.
I was haunted by the fact that I might be unworthy of
the costly schooling God was giving me. I had won a
scholarship in the school of suffering. As Dostoevski said,
"I wanted to be worthy of my sufferings."

Learning only comes through active participation in
the educative process. Had I resigned myself to passiv-
ity, I would have flunked the course in which God had
enrolled me. Ecstasy is the product of believing that
God is in the middle of life, even in its hours of agony
and suffering, and of becoming actively involved in find-
ing out all that this presence promises.

I would never have invited suffering. It is terrifying,
shattering, life-changing. But once you've experienced it,
the new dimensions of life are so profound—the new
sensitivities and the new understandings—that one becomes deeply grateful that God even permits suffering to
come as part of his training.

The secret hidden in suffering is not to let blind fate
master one, but to grasp the offered hand of God and to
find a nail hole there. Suffering then becomes another
avenue for celebrating oneness with Christ, who "for
the joy that was set before him endured the cross, de-
spising the shame, and is seated at the right hand of the
throne of God" (Heb. 12:2).

Over the long haul, however, unless suffering breaks
one open to a sensitivity to the needs of others, it can
render the sufferer a useless, whimpering, self-pitying

37

burden. One ought never again to be as quick to judge a brother or a sister to his or her detriment. Each one endures a private Gethsemane where sweat and blood mingle in agonies that can never be communicated.

I discovered that because of my accident I was more readily able to become the other person, living out Luther's catechetical injunction to "put the best construction" on all the other person does. God gives wells of compassion and understanding out of personal experience so that the pain of another can be sensed and carried and shared.

Jesus demonstrates this. "For we have not a high priest who is unable to sympathize with our weaknesses, but one who in every respect has been tempted as we are, yet without sin" (Heb. 4:15). Two supporting pillars sustain us in this experience: in the verses that precede and follow Heb. 4:15, we find these invitations of the writer, "Since we have . . . Jesus . . . let us hold fast our confession. . . . Let us then with confidence draw near to the throne of grace, that we may receive mercy and find grace to help in time of need."

The experience draws its power to bless others as it rests firmly on these two pillars identified by the writer to the Hebrews. *Since we have this Jesus,* that's the crux! Jesus is *for* you. How then can anything go ultimately wrong? *Therefore,* throughout the suffering, one is enabled to hold fast one's confession, and move wildly and boldly in on the love of God "with confidence."

In spite of all the experiences of grace and the joy of Erling's deliverance from death, the day came when I cursed the ocean.

It was Monday. Just four days after that fateful Thursday. All night long the surf had pounded so loudly that sleep was frightened away. That weekend heavy surf warnings had been posted along the south coast, and the beaches were closed to swimmers. The hurricane off the Mexican coast had teased the sea to a fury, and monstrous foam-mouthed waves clawed in frenzy at the beaches and scooped huge fistfuls of sand back into the water.

Destruction threatened the house trailers that clung to the cliffside below us. Unable to sleep, the children and I had walked down at midnight to watch the angry waters. The dark beach was an inferno. Flashlights and lanterns ineffectively pinpointed the engulfing gloom as the owners of the frail trailers sandbagged the toppling seawalls below their homes. Over the whole scene the odor of skunk musk fouled the air.

On Monday morning, I arose early, slipping out of our hillside trailer as quietly as possible so as not to waken the exhausted children. The sun had not yet dispelled the chill of the night as I drove down the hill to the highway and took a left to the hospital.

As I made the turn into the coastal road, anger against the destructive ocean below overwhelmed me. I pulled over to the shoulder of the road and stopped the car.

A violence of emotion took possession of me, and tears filmed my vision as pent-up rage, resentment, and grief engulfed me. Up to this time I had not cried or lost control, and a strength which was a gift of grace had buoyed me.

But now I got out of the car and ran blindly down to the sand's edge. "I hate you, I hate you," I sobbed. "We always loved you and now look what you've done!"

The sea roared back at me, jeering at my cries, and the seagulls swooped down, shrilly protesting my invasion of their early morning privacy.

"Damn your waves and your storm! Because of you

our whole life has changed! Nothing will ever be the same again!"

Was I really saying all these things out loud, or was I just screaming inside as I ran down the beach? The sand was cold, hard, and unyielding under my feet, and finally I stopped in sheer exhaustion and sat there completely overcome by grief.

If only we could go back in time to last Thursday morning. If only we hadn't gone swimming at that particular moment we would have avoided that particular wave. If only Erling had stayed out of the water. If only . . .

At that moment I resented the ocean, resented Erling for getting hurt, . . . and, O God, I realized, I really resent you for letting it all happen!

No one had worked harder than we had for him. We often had skipped vacations, skipped days off. And now this. We hadn't done anything to deserve this!

Then I remembered Jesus. "He came to his own home, and his own people received him not." And had not even God betrayed him, denying him the comfort of his presence on the cross? I heard the lonely cry, "My God, my God, why hast thou forsaken me?" If a sense of betrayal is the worst suffering of all, then how much suffering had we caused him?

Jesus had been immensely kind to us. He had delivered us from the meaninglessness of life and given us the promise of his presence even in tribulation. Our past history was rich with the evidence of his compassion and healing mercies.

As my ancestral forebears had blamed God in the garden for their own sins by first blaming his creature, the snake, and then by the man's blaming of the woman, so I had really blamed God through my bitterness toward the ocean he had created.

"God, forgive me," and this time my voice was real to my ears, and my tears were warm with repentance.

Peace crept into my heart and I thought of all the happy times we had lived through on that beach and on other Pacific shores. I could never really hate those majestic waters. Their rolling depths were comparable to the love of God—limitless, life-giving, beautiful.

"Thank you for giving me back my husband," I whispered to the sea and to God. And never again in the demanding months to follow was I to doubt his love.

WHAT DO I HAVE TO DO - - BREAK MY NECK?

4 | to become aware of my own family

How wonderful it is to have a support group that's all one's own! I cannot conceive of any loneliness more devastating than being forced to live without being able to name any other human as "my family." My life's deepest riches flow from my family associations. Nothing approaches the preciousness of the persons involved in that company, but I almost had to lose my life to appreciate them in this way.

I had played the part of the average American father, caught up in the work ethic, putting my calling as a pastor above everything else, expecting my family to fit into my schedule. If anything was hammered into me during the six years of my seminary study it was this injunction from Paul to Timothy: "Fulfill your ministry." And in all the ten years of college and seminary education, I cannot recall a paragraph's worth that had anything to say about me as a future husband and father.

In the years of my training these extremely important areas of living drew a great blank. Only out of the give-and-take, the often abrasive, but more often loving, contacts of everyday life and the continued study necessitated by my pastoral counselling of families in trouble did I fill in the void.

But I was still too busy to become deeply involved in family relationships. I was so "lost in my ministry" that I was caught in a trap of my own making. I remember with regret the time I dropped one of my children and my wife off at a hospital before a tonsillectomy and then drove on for a speaking engagement somewhere else. Like many other busy fathers, I was often unable to be present for birthday parties, or was out-of-town when other family celebration times occurred. At graduate school I was so busy getting a degree and at the same time working at part-time jobs that I almost abdicated as a father, leaving Marge to be the sole parent for our three preschoolers.

I was in complete intellectual agreement with the idea that a child needs parents who are available to talk to, listen to, play games with, and to share experiences while they are still fresh and alive. I suppose nothing disturbs me more than my failure to enter as fully as I could have into my children's lives.

"Real fellowship," says Jamie Buckingham, "is . . . coming together like grapes . . . crushed . . . knowing each other's sins and failures and weaknesses . . . with skins of ego broken . . . the rich, fragrant, exhilarating juices of life mingling with the wine of sharing, understanding, accepting, forgiving, and caring. Fellowship is the fusing of personalities in the Presence and Person of Jesus Christ."

In my family I discovered this fellowship in its most meaningful expression as my children repaid a thousand-

43

fold whatever meager fathering I had given them. Very simply and as a matter of record, Kristi saved my life. Erling supported my neck and prevented further injury to my spinal cord. Together with Marge and my assistant pastor, they pulled me out of the waves to safety on the beach. When Steve returned to the beach that day, he came directly to the hospital to join his mother in her long night vigil outside the ICU. Our two married sons and their families came from other towns to give loving support to us. The knowledge of their presence during those long weeks when only family members were permitted to visit brought warmth and joy to me.

All the family relationships that I had taken so for granted before and had done so little to nurture, suddenly became pivotal in keeping me alive. The struggle to return to physical function became fun because of them. To live again with them was worth all the agony it cost and infinitely more. As Nietzsche affirmed, but never really discovered for himself, "He who has a *why* to live can bear with almost any *how*."

Erling is really too hard on himself. It's true that his devotion to his pastoral calling took him away from the family circle a great deal, but the loss was perhaps more his loss than the children's. They were secure in his love and though they coveted more of his time, children have a beautiful way of accepting us as we are.

Perhaps we need to speak more to a social system that demands so much of fathers that there is no time left for family. Or is it our own values that need clarifying so that we are not overburdened by guilt if we don't work ourselves to the point of exhaustion? Have we been so brainwashed by advertisers that our consumer mentality drives us to sacrifice relationships in order to accumulate the means to buy things?

44

A tremendous amount of comfort came to me through our children, and they demonstrated great strength and initiative in assuming responsibilities that set me free to be with Erling and to concentrate on his needs. Kristi immediately took charge of the shopping, cooking, mothering, entertaining, and all household chores. Steve and Erling mowed, watered, helped with mailings, and maintained the cars.

At the same time, it was necessary to remember that the accident had produced certain emotional needs in them, too. Kristi had nightmares for a long time afterwards—nightmares in which she relived the whole rescue experience but in which she lost her father's body to the ocean and would awake in terror.

Gradually, the nightmares became less frequent, but in their place came fears born out of the insecurity of realizing how fragile life is. As she said, "If that can happen to someone who's as strong as Dad, then no one is safe."

A panicky fear of driving on the freeway gripped her, and she became very anxious about my safety. In fact, all of the children became protective of me. They didn't want me to drive alone to the hospital; and I had the feeling that they were always hovering over me as though fearful that I, too, might be snatched away.

At that point, I had to face my own needs and the realization that I could very easily grow to like that kind of attention. Before any crippling dependencies could take permanent shape in our relationships, I decided it was essential to establish my own independence and set them free to be independent also. After a week of being chauffered back and forth to the hospital by one or the other of them and seeing them check schedules to be sure one of them was able to be with me at the hospital every minute, I very firmly let them know that I was just fine and able to be alone occasionally.

Although it's important to come to this point as soon as possible, it's also important not to arrive there too soon. Our youngest son, Erling, had never demonstrated any of the overt hysteria or fears that Kristi had shown. Yet he had gone through the whole experience to the same degree Kristi had. Caught in the pressures of the whole event, I was unable to deal with his needs even though I knew he could not have gone through the accident without it marking him in some way.

About three weeks after his father's hospitalization, he quietly approached me one afternoon just as I had lain down to rest for a while. "Mom, can I talk to you?" he asked in a whisper. "I don't want anyone else to hear, though."

So we talked and he told me that he had such depressed feelings, but he didn't know why. As he poured out these feelings, I saw a relationship between his sense of depression and the hospital rule that no one under sixteen could visit in the ICU. Erling was fourteen. I asked him if it would help him to see his father. At that point he started to cry, apologizing for "being a baby." I assured him that I had thought it strange that he had not cried long before this.

That evening, I explained the situation to the nurse in charge and asked if Erling could have enough time with his father to take care of his emotional need. What they said to each other in ICU is still known only to Erling and his father, but whatever happened, he came out of there totally restored and smiling.

I knew from my years of work with preschool children how important it is to help them work through their feelings when they go through guilt and fear-producing

46

events, but I had not been as sensitive to the needs of a fourteen-year-old who had learned the unfortunate precept of a society which says, "Big boys don't cry"—even when they need to!

We had forgotten about Kimberly, too. Kimberly, our granddaughter, was spending a few days with us at the beach, since a baby brother had been born into their family just the night before the accident. She was playing at the edge of the water when Erling was hurt.

A friend had taken charge of her when the ambulance bore us away, and no one really thought of dealing with Kimmie's emotions at the time, because she, like our son Erling, seemed outwardly undisturbed.

When her father came to take her back home the next day, she was immediately caught up in the excitement of the return of her mother and baby brother from the hospital.

Our first indication that her reactions had not been dealt with came when our son Mike brought his family, baby and all, to the hospital for the occasion of his father's first wheelchair trip during visiting hours. The nurses had told us beforehand that this was to be the day Erling, in his new brace, would be wheeled out to the waiting room so that he could visit with the whole family at one time.

When Kimmie heard her grandfather's voice in the hall, she started to cry and ran terrified into a corner and hid her face. Her mother went over to her and held her but she would not look at Erling at all, keeping her eyes tightly shut all the while he was there.

After the nurse had come to take Erling back to his room, I asked Kimmie if I could talk to her. She climbed into my lap and I said, "I really haven't had a chance to hold you or to talk to you since Grandpa was hurt, and I've really missed you so much."

Kimmie replied, "I was afraid to look at Grandpa."

"You thought he'd look different, didn't you?"

In reply, she asked, "Is his head back on?"

For six-year-old Kimmie a broken neck could only be understood in terms of her dolls, I learned. When dolls have broken necks, their heads come off. I explained to her what it meant for people to have broken necks, asking if anyone in her kindergarten or school had ever had a broken arm or leg. One boy had had a broken arm.

"Did his arm come off when it was broken?" I asked, and we talked at length about broken bones, and Kimmie felt the bones in the back of her neck and my neck.

Children fear mutilation almost more than death, and the thought of seeing her grandfather in some hideous distortion of himself was very frightening to Kimmie. She needed to be reassured by all of us that he didn't look any different except for the brace he wore and the short hair growing out after his head shave.

Kimmie may also have had some vague feelings of guilt about her grandfather's injury since she hadn't been able to help him in any way when he was hurt. While all the other people had been busy doing one thing or another for him at that time, Kimmie had probably been taken aside so that she wouldn't be "in the way." Her anxiety was further increased by the screaming ambulance and the fact that her last glimpse of her grandfather was of him being rushed off on the stretcher with the lifeguard holding a collar around his neck to immobilize it, leaving a crowd of frightened, crying, and worried people behind.

Following that, her mother and father had been busy with the new baby, and I was totally absorbed with other matters at the hospital. So Kimmie had been forgotten.

The whole matter resolved itself quite simply for her.

After the first wheelchair incident, Mike and Barbie, his wife, took turns visiting Erling in his room while one of them stayed with the children in the waiting room. The day came when her parents felt she was ready to see her grandfather again. Without warning her and without any great fanfare, Mike wheeled his father out to the lobby where Kimmie was busily at work coloring. She looked up as they came through the door. All it took was that one look. "Hi, Grandpa!" she said.

Then she ran over to him, impulsively put her head against his arm and said, "I love you, Grandpa." After that she accepted him, brace and all, and apparently had no further problems.

At the time Kristi turned me over in the water, my words were, "Call Mom." Those two words describe a relationship. My first thought and the cry of my heart was to have her come to me. Even in my moment of crisis, I knew that if she came everything would be taken care of, everything would somehow be all right *for me.*

"Call Mom." Marge had earned the right to this kind of dependency on my part. From the first moment I met her, I loved her, not only for her beauty but also because I recognized in her a strength that could match my own. I had never needed her strength more than I did that day when I lost all of my own. I needed someone to take charge of me, and I knew of no one else who would suffice.

When she responded to Kristi's call and I saw her in the water beside me, I relaxed knowing that she was there. On the beach she knelt beside me and whispered, "Everything's going to be all right. I love you."

And I trusted her. I marvel that in the weeks to follow I was never troubled by the possibility that I might be permanently paralyzed, permanently hospitalized, or permanently separated from her in any way, once I had been saved from death. The enormity of my trust in her can only be measured up against the fact that the other two much younger men with me in ICU were still paralyzed when I came into the unit, even though they had been in the hospital one and two weeks before I came.

A trust relationship is the result of much experience. I had learned through many years of marriage that Marge was worthy of my trust.

When disaster strikes, all that one has been programmed to do by experience and training becomes operative. In a mechanical, almost robot-like manner, we play the part for which life has rehearsed us. My brief stint as a student nurse, the first-aid courses, the years of dealing with family and congregational crises, the practice of immediate turning to God for help—all of these factors become part of one's automatic response to catastrophe.

I tried not to let my emotional reaction to Erling's apparent paralysis affect my objective appraisal of his situation. I was terrified at his helplessness. When you see someone you love as much as your own life—someone who's always been so strong and vibrantly alive—lying inert and blue in the water, the situation is almost incomprehensible.

What motivated me to be all that I needed to be in that moment was the look in Erling's eyes when I reached him in the water. They fastened on my face with such mute trust and love that I could not let him down. I didn't know until much later that he had told Kristi to call me, but I sensed his absolute dependence on my actions for his help.

All of this was communicated to me by his eyes. When two persons have lived together in complete inti-

macy for almost thirty years, there are sure to be certain frequencies on which contact is made without words. I understood Erling's need for reassurance and sensed that something unbelievably beyond description had happened to him in the water. It was all written in his eyes.

If my eyes communicated anything to Marge, they were also saying thanks for an up-to-date relationship. All friendships that matter cost something in effort. Cheap love is no more a possibility than cheap discipleship. To keep married love alive requires infinite watchfulness. The demonic rift that separates all persons from God fights to separate husband and wife as well.

Marriage lives by the daily forgiveness of sins. Our marriage was no different in this respect; our relationship too was built on daily forgiveness and renewal.

During the process of getting ready for that much-needed two-week vacation, we had been so busy making sure that our responsibilities at church and day nursery were taken care of that we had lost touch with each other. We had come upon one of those dry periods in a marriage when communication breaks down and the marriage bed seems a mile wide. Who knows how these ruptured relationships start? Was it her fault or my fault? In any event for a few days we had lost closeness, and the demon of pride moved in to keep the rift a reality.

Before going into the water that Thursday afternoon, I got up from the beach towel on which I'd been relaxing and told Marge I was going to run for a while.

I had only run a hundred yards or so when I heard her voice calling over the wind, "Do you want someone to run with?"

I turned and saw her running toward me and knew

that she was saying to me, "Let's forget whatever it is that's between us and just love each other."

I held out my hand and when she caught up with me we started to run together not saying a word. We were almost at Scotchman's Cove when we turned back, walking hand in hand and making some plans for the evening. When we got back to the place where we'd started, Marge went to sit with her friend and I went into the water, released and joyous in our restored relationship.

Someone's got to make the first move. It wasn't always me, but how grateful I have been that the Spirit nudged me to make the first move that day.

Times of tension are sure to come whenever two human beings are trying to work at the business of living together and this is part of the growing process. The important thing is to live in perpetual sensitivity to God's Spirit as he convicts and renews, and then not to be disobedient! I'm sure that a large portion of the grace that sustained both of us through the crisis came because we had just experienced that outpouring of it which always follows an encounter with forgiveness.

It takes grace to say, "I'm sorry," and grace to respond with forgiveness, and both persons are blessed in the process. Maybe that's essentially what married love is all about.

I've never felt that it was up to the wife to always make the first move toward healing, as some advocates of an authority/submission relationship affirm. There's so much misunderstanding today—both among Christians and non-Christians—about the relationship of husband and wife, that it's important for all who understand what freedom in Christ means to speak to this issue.

Some who never experience what Christ's "freedom"

means keep talking about "orders" and "authority" and perpetuate a relationship which is legalistic and completely against the mind of the New Testament. The New Testament stance is servanthood, and that means that each person in any Christian relationship, including marriage, is to be *subject* or *submissive to the other* (Eph. 5:21). Granted, sometimes it's necessary for one mate to be totally submissive to the other, even if the other does not respond in kind, if that other one is an unbeliever or not yet mature in Christ, in order to win him or her for Christ. But that is not the norm for a marriage of equally dedicated followers of Jesus. In this situation each partner is under orders to "be humble, thinking of others as better than yourself," and thus having the "mind of Christ" (Phil. 2:3). The masculine "need" for authority and power is totally at variance with the servant stance of Christ!

Love, freely won and freely given, produces behavior in each spouse that the law—which is so often invoked to force the other into stereotyped roles of responsibility —can never motivate. Marge perfectly unveiled this for me when she gave herself in a total abandonment of devotion to me and to my needs. Not only did she stay close to me in the hospital so that I was comforted by her presence, but she anticipated and answered all of my spoken and unspoken needs. When I came home from the hospital, she performed all those functions which my paralyzed arms and hands could not do for themselves.

Love frees the other person to become all that he or she can be in Christ. We had always been concerned about each other's wholeness. When Erling came home from the hospital, I knew that his ultimate return to wholeness depended on my freeing him to grow.

So I informed him that his homecoming gift from me was to be the opportunity to feed himself! For the two months of his hospitalization either the nurses or I had fed him. He had never picked up one morsel of food by himself. He had never been able to bring his hand up to his mouth. We made jokes about his needing to have someone else scratch his nose!

The night he came home and sat down to eat, I tied a large dishtowel around his neck, put his plate of food on another towel on the table, and told him that he had been fed his last meal and that now he was on his own. Eating was a struggle for him, and my children thought I was being excessively mean to their father, but from that time on Erling fed himself!

The other's growth must always be the chief concern of a marriage partner. Only love cares enough to make that its aim. Crippling dependency relationships must not be fostered or cherished by either husband or wife.

Women are no better and no worse than men at this. All of us are oriented to self, and it takes the dynamite power of the Holy Spirit to crack that self-serving, self-preserving shell and open us up to love. Women and men are equally adept at destroying the other person if love does not control. The difference may be only in the learning of techniques. Men are taught to destroy more openly; women more subtly.

But each one has the same possibility of becoming a new creation in Christ Jesus and able, through him, to relate to each other's wholeness.

I have long felt that too many discussions of marriage and family roles have been carried out in the bitter separating atmosphere of the fall into sin as described in Genesis 3. That chapter is filled with harsh recriminations—man against woman, woman against man, both against God. So often the tension in marriage that turns them into a "horror story" grows out of the Fall depicted there.

God originally intended something so different for women and men. He made humans, the record states in Genesis 1:27, male and female, without other qualification. Each had the same responsibility toward his creation. They were to relate to each other in mutual interdependency. The job of "helping" the male is given to the woman, and this role is one of empowering, not assisting.

Those who are related to Jesus are dedicated to eradicating all traces of the brokenness of Genesis 3 and to restoring the wholeness originally intended by God for his people.

The sexual act is part of this wholeness and basic to marriage. Normal marriage is incomplete without sex. "The two shall become one flesh," was God's only description of this union. The self-giving abandonment of each one to the other in the sexual act is the deepest means of knowing each other. When two people work at responding to the other's love-making, the marriage is in the process of continual renewal.

My accident could have radically changed all sexual relationship for us. I was aware that I had no normal sexual sensations during my hospitalization. Paralysis had made me impotent. Somehow the fact of this never bothered me in the hospital, even though our sexual relationship had always been a deeply satisfying one. Apparently I never doubted my full restoration and anticipated that a return to normal sexual function would be part of that.

It wasn't until later that I learned that spinally injured husbands are more concerned with regaining sexual potency than they are even with walking.

The fact that we might never again be able to make love did bother me. I began to understand how women who have had a satisfying sexual life must feel when they are suddenly widowed or divorced. It must be difficult enough to deal with sexual needs when one has never had the dependable sex of marriage, but to have known this as a regular part of one's life and then to lose it in one traumatic moment leaves a gaping hunger that can never be satisfied in the same way again.

Days without one's mate are dreary enough, but nights deprived of the constant comfort of the other's presence are unbearable. Flesh is torn from flesh and suffering results.

I felt that we would have to work out an entirely new pattern of relating to each other as sexual human beings if Erling were to remain impotent. The neurosurgeon asked me to make an appointment with him for the purpose of discussing Erling's situation. As we talked about his progress, he also explained to me that there were signs that Erling was regaining sensation throughout his body and was responding well to the pin-prick tests which were administered regularly. This meant that bowel and bladder control would probably return and with it sexual function.

We rejoiced together when I discussed what the doctor had said with Erling. To be able to look forward again to the wholeness of loving was a great gift.

Shalom is a word of great significance. It's the Hebrew word for "peace" but it has meaning for human relationships which are left unexpressed by that word. *Shalom*-peace is found in being together, in relating to family, clan, and others in wholeness. Separation is dis-peace (not *shalom*).

Our family is now *shalom*. We are together in new ways. Because I almost lost them, I cannot get enough of being with them now. I need their *shalom*.

5 | to drain power from the promises of god

For ten days no food passed my lips, and for another week after that I had only liquid nourishment, but physical hunger was never a problem for me as long as I was hospitalized. Later on I forced myself to eat at the insistence of the staff.

My real hunger was for the reality of God as he unveils himself through the words of the Bible. Words that I had stored in my memory kept surfacing to sustain me. The three verses that had special significance through the changing periods of my life returned to nourish me. As a child I fell in love with the realism of the promise of Jesus to his friends in Bethany, "I am the resurrection and the life; he that lives and believes in me shall never die" (John 11:25). Because death was so pressingly real in our little town and because I had to learn to live with those tolling funeral bells in the church tower next to my home, the promise of this resurrection event gave life to my spirit.

In the troubled and lonely moments of my adolescent years, I discovered a fulfillment of the promises of Jesus, "I will never leave you nor forsake you. . . . No one shall ever snatch you out of my hand." In the days when I found it difficult to communicate with my own father, I reveled in the warmth and intimacy of a personal relationship with the Lord which this promise gave. I rejoiced in it! It wasn't that my father didn't care for me and his other children. I sensed his pride when we achieved and I was aware of his expectations that we would live honestly and decently, but he never articulated his feelings for us in any way nor did he demonstrate any affection. His basic philosophy of fatherhood was to provide food, shelter, and clothing, and this he did faithfully.

My father's basic personal drive was work. Work was my inheritance from him and I reproduced his drive in my own life. I exulted in the vitality that throbbed in my being when I worked. I lived up to every one of his expectations for me when it came to output of energy. His very life underscored Paul's injunction that only they who work should have a right to eat. My muscles, always in good shape, agreed with him. So we could work side by side as he painted houses, bought grain, managed his grain elevator, and feel a sense of oneness as I matched my energy to his energy.

A certain kind of intimacy was ours, but as a child and a young man I longed for more. I wanted my father to put his arms around me, to hear him say, "I love you, Erling," and I wanted him to talk to me about those troubling subjects that make growing up such a lonely business. But this wasn't part of his background or nature. Although his eyes sometimes communicated approval and affection, his Scandinavian reserve kept us at a distance.

Even if my father had been everything that I thought a father should be, he still could not have met all my needs. No human being can ever fully meet the needs of another human being. Not even the most sensitive marriage relationship can provide each mate with all that he or she needs for total happiness. At some point we fail each other, no matter how hard we try not to fail. No one person can be all things to another person.

So there remains in us that lonely core of being that longs for affirmation; for someone to reach the essential *me*. In this longing lies so much of the fear of death—the fear that the *me* shall vanish into nothingness without ever having been discovered and affirmed.

With youthful delight, I sensed the mystical presence of Jesus in his promise that he would never leave me nor forsake me. I realized his constant presence, knowing me, understanding me, speaking to my deepest longing for affection and understanding. The Word was made flesh and lived with me.

In the awesome demands of adulthood, even muscle energy was not enough. When life stretched me taut and required more than human energy can provide, a thousand times I experienced power in the same way Paul did, "I can do all things through Christ who keeps on pouring his power into me." I had to claim this as my own personal promise in my particular times of need.

The promises of God must enter one's life. Mouthing words of Scripture can become a cheap process, as Clarence Jordan in his Cottonpatch version of Romans 2:13, says, "It is not those who listen to scripture but those who act on scripture who will be considered right with God." Perhaps physical and emotional helplessness provides less hindrance for the promises to seep through muscles and sinews and cells until they are re-formed in changed attitudes and perspectives.

60

Stored-up experiences with the Word can be amazingly supportive in moments of sudden need. I caressed words that I had memorized across the years and drained from them a strange miraculous power. In those days when my hands could not hold a book and Marge could not be with me long enough to spend much time reading, the words in my mind were the food that kept me alive.

Of one thing I am more convinced than before. You've got to know the Book *before* tragedy strikes!

Physical energy was the name of the game for me following Erling's accident. My need for strength increased in inverse ratio to Erling's decrease. Sleep time was cut to a minimum as the demands of each day grew. Travel to and from the hospital consumed hours of each day. Responsibility for directing the preschool day nursery at our church was still mine even though my staff members assumed much of it. New enrollees needed interviewing, and payroll checks had to be written. Fall schedules demanded deadline attention. Correspondence spiraled. Insurance forms demanded data-gathering. Some appointments needed to be cancelled and others made. Long distance phone calls were urgent. Emotional uncertainties drained psychic resources. Responsibility for so many other lives and so many decisions pressed me on all sides.

Occasionally I was oppressed by remembering how many people were depending on me for emotional support: children, relatives, Erling's aged mother, families whose children were at the day nursery, members of the congregation, and above all Erling himself. The need to cope was inescapable.

Who is sufficient for all these things? I joined the

millions of other humans for whom life suddenly demands more than human strength can bear.

Just as the relationships of Erling's childhood had created the "working fool" in him, so my childhood had molded me into the perennial "big sister." As the oldest girl in a family of eight children, I had been forced into a position of feeling responsible for helping everyone else who was hurting in any way. So I suffered under the hurts of my children whose father had almost died, of a congregation who loved him and depended on him, of people everywhere who knew Erling as God's servant and needed help with a faith suddenly called into question by his accident.

And in the hospital waiting room, a whole new set of needs demanded "big-sistering." I entered into the lives of women whose husbands were brought in with heart attacks; of a man whose wife had attempted suicide with his sleeping pills and whose three adolescent children had run away from home in protest; of a young woman whose father had died a month before and whose mother was dying next to Erling in the ICU; and above all I was totally caught up in the family needs of the other paralyzed persons.

Power and strength came to me from several sources, all of them comprehended in the Word of God. As Erling has expressed it, there were the "words" tucked away in my "heart." The Spirit spotlighted them as needed.

Often the words were those of old hymns, long fallen into disuse, but called out of oblivion by the Spirit to meet my needs: "In Jesus I find rest and peace. / The world is full of sorrow; / His wounds are my abiding place; / Let the unknown tomorrow / Bring what it may, / There I can stay, / My faith finds all I need today, / I will not trouble borrow."

Fragments of scripture drifted in and out of my consciousness as I sat, drove, visited, worked. "Lo, I am with you always. . . . I have loved you with an everlasting love. . . . I will not leave you orphans. . . . I have overcome the world. . . . In him is the victory. . . . Peace I leave with you." The words came and went, and they blessed me.

In ways totally indefinable, Jesus, the Word made flesh, was very real. I recognized that the Holy Spirit was again giving birth to the Babe of Bethlehem in my life. The Incarnation, while a historical reality, is also a present fact, as the Word is reincarnated every day in the world of each individual's living. His biography is constantly being written again in the historical realities of each day, and as I lost myself in the world of the Spirit, I celebrated the Gospel according to Marge Wold, my own personal kerygma.

With little time to read the written pages of the Book, I was heavily dependent on the fellowship of believers to keep new input coming from the Word. Recently a letter came from a widowed friend in which this statement was written, "I will never forget the scripture passage you quoted when I needed it most, 'As your days, so shall your strength be' (Deut. 33:25). This has helped me immeasurably as I try my best in daily duties." I could write thousands of letters saying the same thing over and over. I remember the card that came with the words printed large on the front of it, "My strength is made perfect in weakness," and I recall the strengthened leaping of my heart when I saw it. How I thanked God for the sender! The quoting of scripture sometimes seems trite and superfluous, but given in love it always blesses.

Even though the actual words of scripture might never be articulated, the Word was always made flesh in and through the physical form of people. In the sec-

ond chapter of Acts, we are told that the Holy Spirit came upon all flesh in a fulfillment of Joel's prophecy, and I came to believe that in a new way. God's Spirit ministers through the likely people and the unlikely ones, and all whose lives touched mine in love throughout those demanding days were God's ministering angels to me.

God will not unveil the glory of his word to professional "hacks." Too many use the words of the Bible as weapons to clobber others into their particular bias or as barricades behind which they fortify themselves. There they load their little pea-shooters and shoot away gleefully at their real or imaginary antagonists. Religious folk can be the worst offenders.

The Bible is written to provide a relationship with Jesus. All relationships that are to be kept intimate and alive demand fresh communication. New contacts must be established with the Word each day as needs change. God communicates himself in these human communication symbols called "words." A word, a phrase, a sentence perhaps in a new translation leaps out and won't let go until you come alive with a new glimpse of his nature. He fills your mind with that other drumbeat which demands obedience to its rhythms.

The marvel is that the formless, frameless Word of God comes through the printed page.

It wasn't long before the remembered passages were insufficient to satisfy my growing hunger for new encounters with the Word in print. To satisfy my appetite my son Steve printed words of the Bible on letter-size pieces of cardboard that could be hung on the hook of a Murphy stand next to my bed. Every day Marge brought a new card and I devoured it with my eyes and with my spirit.

64

But the portion of scripture that will always be associated for me with this chapter of my life is Psalm 34. No other section of the Bible sustained me to the same extent this did. I identified with these remarkable words of one who had, thousands of years before me, found God forever worthy of praise. The words became my words, and I thought about them day and night:

"I will praise the Lord no matter what happens. I will constantly speak of his glories and grace. I will boast of all his kindness to me. Let all who are discouraged take heart. Let us praise the Lord together, and exalt his name.

"For I cried to him and he answered me! He freed me from all my fears. Others too were radiant at what he did for them. Theirs was no downcast look of rejection! This poor man cried to the Lord —and the Lord heard him and saved him out of his troubles. For the Angel of the Lord guards and rescues all who reverence him.

"Oh, put God to the test and see how kind he is! See for yourself the way his mercies shower down on all who trust in him. If you belong to the Lord, reverence him; for everyone who does this has everything he needs. Even strong young lions sometimes go hungry, but those of us who reverence the Lord will never lack any good thing. . . .

"The Lord is close to those whose hearts are breaking; he rescues those who are humbly sorry for their sins. The good man does not escape all troubles—he has them too. But the Lord helps him in each and every one. God even protects him from accidents" (Ps. 34:1-10, 18-20 LB).

The Word must mingle with individual experience

to really come alive. It demands one's full attention, even physical involvement. Only then do the words disclose their secrets, refusing to give them up to the casual reader.

A parable of involvement with the Word was re-enacted for me at the time the tongs were removed from my head. The Stryker frame on which I lay was an ingenious device which permitted me to be turned periodically. After two hours on my back, the nurses turned me over, sandwiched between the top and bottom of the frame, and made me lie for an hour face downward, chin and forehead supported by straps, my face looking down at a small platform under the "bed." That face-down hour was an especially tortured period. Breathing was more difficult, life-support hoses were in danger of being pinched off and the chinstrap always seemed to be on the edge of my chin ready to slip down my neck and strangle me.

To make that hour bearable, Marge also put a copy of Psalm 34 on the little platform a foot or so below my face so that I could read it in that prone position. (Normally, the platform was used to hold an emesis basin in the event that the patient needed to expectorate.) The paper was there the day the doctor came to remove the tongs after I had been fitted with a metal neck brace. I was lying face down and as he removed the tongs, I read the words, "This poor man cried to the Lord—and the Lord heard him and saved him out of his troubles," and as I read drops of blood came from the holes in my skull and fell on the paper where I was reading.

Experience mingled with the words makes the Word come alive.

Bible study can become a mere juggling of words and phrases unless it results in a meeting with God himself.

66

I have participated in study groups where there is much learned discussion about the meanings of verses and individual words and where there is a great deal of historical and philosophical information exchanged. Much learning is evidenced, but when the discussion is over, the whole affair has only been a stimulating academic experience. The voice of God had had little opportunity to break into the conversation, and the words served only to veil his presence.

Imagine my delight when I was moved into a less restricted section of ICU, and I was permitted the luxury of a tape recorder! My son Erling spent hours recording the Gospel according to St. John and segments of other biblical books. With some of his own records playing while he read, he had added a musical background that intensified the meanings of the words. At late night hours and when sleep failed me, the nurse would put the earpiece into my ear, turn on the machine, and my son's young voice enunciated the old familiar message in the new words of the Living Bible. Though paralyzed in body, I walked the highways of Palestine in the Spirit with my Lord.

6 | to explore the dimensions of prayer

When our eldest son had reached a certain point of sophomoric wisdom, he puzzled, "Mom, I can't understand how people as smart as you and Dad can really believe prayer does any good!"

John has long since outgrown his uncertainties, but perhaps his puzzlement is found to some degree in all of us. A belief in the efficacy of prayer does seem incompatible with intelligent, rational perception of the reality of life as it is.

We admit at the outset of this chapter on prayer that we are not sophisticates in this area. We simply believe in prayer as talking to God. Techniques, styles, forms of prayer have never engaged our attention. Inquiry into "right" or "wrong" ways of praying has never interested us; we simply pray.

A life of experience had led us to believe that God hears and answers prayer.

"Prayer is helplessness." That phrase from Hallesby's classic book on prayer kept drumming its way into my brain those holy nights that I lay awake in the hospital. Prayer *is* helplessness. I realized with pain that too often I had looked on prayer as a rheumy-eyed beggar stumbling around ineffectually. How often I had read those statements about Jesus praying all night before he made his major decisions such as the calling of his associates, and yet I did not follow him in that practice. How often I had encouraged others to pray, only to discover that my own prayer life was a shallow mockery.

It wasn't that I hadn't prayed. I had faithfully risen before the other members of the family for years to search for God's will in his book and through prayer, but prayer had become perfunctory and routine. I could converse easily with my Lord, clothing petitions with fluent phrases. But prayer is the expression of a deep personal relationship with God, and through the years I was aware that my relationship with him had lost intensity.

The sudden helplessness of paralysis brought me back to the place where the meaning in the rest of Hallesby's statement on prayer could find expression in my life. The complete sentence reads, "Prayer is helplessness *that asks Jesus to come in and to take over.*"

The meaning of this for me is vividly articulated in a tape recording made by Marge as I talked one evening in ICU. It was a message from me which she was to bring to my congregation at the next Sunday service:

"I've always loved Jesus. I was baptized into his family as a little baby. I loved him all my life. In confirmation he became very close. In the beginning of my ministry I knew how much I loved him, and I offered him my life and all that I had and

69

I really wanted him to matter. For me life has been Jesus Christ. He's been my passion, my love, and the one to whom I owe my whole ministry.

"In the last dozen years or so things have begun to press in. I read such passages as Revelation 2:4 where Jesus warns about love growing cold. I didn't feel that my love was growing cold, but I knew that I was beginning to be an administrator and a sharer of external things and that oftentimes the pressure of the every day stole away the right of the priority of Jesus in my own devotional life, in my own witness life, in my whole life with Jesus as Lord of my living. It deeply bothered me so that during that period I longed to break through any kind of a wall and to be back again in the warmth and wonder of knowing who he is and what he is like and what he can do. And I prayed secretly that he would make this known to me.

"Hundreds of times I've asked him, 'When you teach me this lesson, don't touch my family. You just tell me because I've got to know!'

"Years are so few. Ministry closes so quickly and contacts that have to be made have to count, but I knew that at times I wasn't transmitting, that at times I didn't live in that intimacy that made Christ a transparency. And it deeply bothered me, and I kept praying inside myself, 'My Lord, I know your grace and that you give gifts to beggars, and I want this gift more than anything else.'

"So when a nurse asked me, 'Do you feel any resentment?' all I can say is, 'God forbid, all I feel is grace!' I have never known such grace in all of my life. It's an experience so inexpressible that I feel like what Paul writes in the Corinthian letter of being in the seventh heaven and seeing things

70

that he couldn't explain. And it's so personal and so intimate and so real and so possible for everyone that I want to share this experience with you.

"It's hard to explain what I mean. I wake sometimes at two o'clock in the morning when pain comes because of a frame that encircles my head. I wake at two and three and four in the morning and I start thinking about my Lord and thinking about what he means to me and I begin weeping. I have wept more in three weeks than I have wept in all of my life, but every one has been a tear of joy. Sometimes I think of him and I shudder and convulse in just sheer ecstasy over his kindness that he answered my prayer.

"He didn't have to shake me up and answer the inmost sob, 'Jesus, I want to be yours as I've never been before,' but in his infinite kindness he stops me and teaches me the most important lessons and has given me the most important schooling that I have ever had.

"Everything I've ever lived for is *real!* But I haven't tapped it as I ought and I want to make confession to you this morning, and I want to make you understand as I've never made you understand before what's available to you as it has been made available to me. And it's available without shattering experience because God just wants to give gifts. That's what it's all about. God so loved the world that he gave his Son, and with his Son he gives every gift anybody could ever want and he surprises us with such intimacy of mercy that you just get shaken.

"And when you begin to take time to lie back and do what he asks us to do, 'Be still and know that I am God,' you discover that he's real.

"So I don't want anyone to say, 'I'm sorry for Pastor Wold.' I want you to say, 'I'm glad, profoundly glad, for a God so big that he even answers prayer when he doesn't have to, and makes us experience the very things he's promised through Jesus Christ.'

"It's this that makes life so wonderful, so surpassingly beautiful, that I can lie here at night and just sing his praise and adore him from the deeps of me!"

I played this taped message at a morning worship service just a month after Erling's accident as part of the talk I was invited to give that Sunday. I had had to stop the recorder frequently during the taping session in ICU to give him time to recover emotional control but even so the message was punctuated by the broken sounds of a strong man crying.

My talk centered that morning about the healing power of tears. In all our 30 years of marriage I had never seen Erling cry. I had often marveled at his apparent composure at funerals, weddings, family crises, and celebrations, and at all those other occasions when emotion reduces most of us to tears and nose-blowings. I cried easily, especially at baptisms and weddings! Here then was a complete reversal. I never shed one tear during or after the accident (except for my brief explosion at the storm-mad ocean), and now Erling wept easily. Granted he was weak and shocked by the trauma he had suffered, but his tears were of a different nature. Never were they tears of self-pity, of loss, of anger, or resentment. They flowed whenever he tried to express what Jesus meant to him or whenever he spoke of the goodness of God.

Not once did I feel that his tears put him in a posi-

tion of weakness. To me he had never seemed more strong, and I rejoiced in the honest emotion the tears symptomized. Tears are part of our nature and somehow never to cry had always seemed to me a betrayal of wholeness.

Wherever I played the tape during the months following—and invitations came from Bible classes, midweek meetings, business groups—the message always produced an openness of response such as nothing else Erling had ever said had done. Hearts were touched, spontaneous rededications of lives occurred, and severed relationships were mended. Healings of body and spirit followed. Because of Erling's honesty, others became boldly honest, and the Spirit was not hindered.

I played the tape at a retreat for pastors' wives and afterwards several of them sought me out alone to confide, "My husband has often felt the same longing for renewal and a return to his first love. But does God need to break our necks to accomplish this?"

Perhaps he does, I thought.

For some time I had sensed that my husband's joy in his work had worn thin. The routines of the ministry that he loved had grown trite. Preaching was still easy for him, and it still had a profound effect on people's lives since Erling could never be anything but totally wholehearted about his love for God and for people. It wasn't that his faith had grown dim or that he was any less convinced of the validity of all that he was preaching and saying and doing. But somehow the shine had worn off. The tarnish of daily-ness had dimmed the experience of being a pastor.

Whatever the cause, his "problem" bothered me, too. I knew there was nothing I could say or do that would make the situation any better for him. I resisted the urge to mouth pious platitudes or to become patronizing-

73

ly helpful. I had sense enough to recognize that renewing the human spirit is a matter for the Holy Spirit. Anyway, what can one say that would help? Most such attempts are about as effective as the following: "How come you're not as close to the Lord as you used to be?" or "It seems like there's something wrong with your spiritual life!"

We immediately recognize how ludicrous such statements are, but sometimes our pious meddlings are just as un-funny and just as harmful in their effect. Imagine what such subtleties do to the one who is suffering enough as it is? If we believe at all in the power of intercessory prayer, then that alone can be of any help to those we love at times like this. And our concern may have to be very quiet and unobtrusive lest it increase the sense of inadequacy and despair the other feels.

Perhaps Erling's despair grew out of some gnawing uncertainty that prayer and reading and all of the spiritual exercises were not effective for him any more. Maybe all of it was just part of the process of growing older, a kind of middle-aged slump. The dreams of youth have not been realized, and the older one grows, the less likely their realization seems.

For a number of years then I had given myself over to prayer for Erling since he had communicated in both verbal and non-verbal ways his desire for renewal. Had I known what would have to happen to restore him to the joy of his Lord, I wonder if I would have persisted in my prayer for his restoration.

But whenever we pray, we are accepting the price tag that might be attached to our prayers. The cost for Erling has been very dear: exceeding pain, the most certain inner agony of knowing that one is helpless, perhaps even a claustrophobic panic over a situation where no matter how much one wills to move, one cannot. Nothing of this was outwardly evident in his behavior in the hospital, and perhaps I just projected my own feelings onto him. But certainly the cost has been a fantastic price to pay for renewal.

For me the cost of answered prayer has been the disruption of a life together so sweet and joyous in its intimacy that I cannot conceive of a marriage relationship any better than ours has been. During those first critical weeks when I could take no food because my dear one was suffering and when only the grace of God sustained me, the deep chill of an unutterable loneliness gripped me only to be replaced by the same ecstasy Erling was experiencing in the realization that here was an answer to our prayers. In that knowledge, I was totally convinced that the best days of his ministry and the best years of our life together lay ahead of us.

As I listened to my tape months after I had left the hospital, I was mystified by what God had finally been able to accomplish in me. We know our need to be broken open, but pride inhibits us with rationalizations that seem to make sense but never really satisfy, "Why expose yourself to ridicule? People won't respect you if you reveal any weakness! Leaders are expected to be above human failings. Think what might happen if you leave yourself too vulnerable to misunderstanding!"

So the need to be honest often passes unexpressed, and we drift along wearing our masks of self-sufficiency until the hammer of God's love smashes us open and tears away our disguises.

It hurts to be exposed as we really are. We male humans especially are conditioned by our culture to hide our weaknesses, to never reveal our emotions if they show any tendency to make us seem less than strong, to never let oneself go in a wild abandonment of self-giving either to God or another human being.

Therefore I reveled at what God could do in spite of me in making me into a transparency of his grace! At least in that moment I was free to be what God wanted me to be.

7 | to experience an invasion of pure grace

As I pondered this marvel, I acknowledged an invasion of pure grace. My helplessness became the door through which the Spirit of Jesus walked in, and I was freed to finally lock myself in without reservation on the promises of God. Like a barnacle that fastens itself tenaciously to any marine surface, I gripped those prayer promises that drifted back onto the shores of my consciousness:

"Whatever you ask in my name, I will do it, that the Father may be glorified in the Son; if you ask anything in my name, I will do it" (John 14:13-14).

"If you abide in me, and my words abide in you, ask whatever you will, and it shall be done for you" (John 15:7).

77

"Truly, truly, I say to you, if you ask anything of the Father, he will give it to you in my name . . . ask, and you will receive, that your joy may be full" (John 16:23-24).

My heart reveled in the contrapuntal music of these prayer themes. Every part is melodically complete and supportive of the other, but the whole becomes a matchless symphony of sound in which the Spirit of God wraps himself. These sub-themes—that the Father may be glorified in the Son, and my words abide in you, that your joy may be full—led me into an insight into the wholeness of prayer.

There's no question about God making himself available. He has opened his heart and made himself totally vulnerable through the cross. He has pledged himself, through his promises, to respond to any of the prayers we bring. When we say, "My prayers never seem to rise higher than the ceiling," let us be aware that there are no ceilings which can separate us from the loving heart of God.

But the wholeness of prayer that became clear to me lay in the realization that prayer is really a dialog between God and the person.

I pray, "God, heal me, please!"

He responds, "If this is the way in which the Father may be glorified in the Son. . . ."

I come back at him, "Okay, God, if you want me to stay this way, then I accept it."

God ties in again, "My will is that your joy may be full."

I become excited by what I am beginning to see, "Then death, recovery, paralysis, whatever, as long as you are with me, Lord!"

God meets me, "As you are abiding in me, my words abide in you."

I discovered this awesome secret that God bends to me as I bend to him. Like the brilliant daring of Abraham who kept such prayer persistence with God that he really pinned God to the mat. God promised to change his plan to destroy the Sin Cities because of Abraham's prayer. Moses "stood in the breach" and God changed his mind about destroying the Israelites (Ps. 106:23). Through dialog in prayer, God and I come to a meeting of minds.

God is the perfect communicator. He not only speaks, but he listens; he not only listens, but he speaks. And this dialog is all intertwined in beautiful counterpoint with the soaring theme, *he cares.*

God's answers to the dilemmas of our lives are often locked up in mysteries that are unveiled to us only in persisting prayer. In essence, God asks us, "Do you care enough to hang on in prayer?"

God links persistence in prayer with the fact of faith. "And he told them a parable, to the effect that they ought always to pray and not lose heart." (Lk. 18:1 ff.) And Jesus proceeds to tell the story of the woman who kept coming to the judge to ask him to vindicate her against her adversary so much that he finally agreed because she was wearing him out and getting on his nerves! So Jesus promises, "If even an evil judge can be worn down like that, don't you think that God will surely give justice to his people who plead with him day and night? Yes! He will answer them quickly!" (LB) Then he ties prayer that "hangs on" to faith, "But the question is: When I, the Messiah, return, how many will I find who have faith [and are praying]?" (Lk. 18:8 LB)

For almost a year God had locked up the answer to a disturbing question in our lives. I had received the call to be Executive Director of the Women's auxiliary of the American Lutheran Church, with headquarters in Minneapolis. Both of us were convinced that this was a call from God to me, but the problems in accepting it seemed insurmountable. How could I accept a position that would separate me from my family by 2000 miles? Granted, our youngest child was now in high school, but all of my training and personal conviction argued against being away from my family for long periods at a time.

But every time I sat down to write declining the job offer, I was prevented from mailing the letter. I set deadlines for a definite answer to prayer, I "put out fleeces" in the style of Gideon (Judges 6:36 ff.), but still no answer except "Go!" and still no resolution to the problems involved.

The day came when the uncertainty bothered me so much that I prayed, "God, I can't stand this indecision any longer. I'm just going to have to say no in order to get some peace." Then came the very clear answer, after months of persisting prayer, that I was going to need the job because I would have to support the family, that something was going to happen to my husband. I didn't doubt at all that this was the Lord speaking to my spirit, but I was deeply troubled and sought counsel from two Christian friends. One was the president of the national auxiliary who had signed the letter calling me to the executive position, and the other was a member of our congregation. Their comfort and fellowship helped me.

When Erling's accident occurred, I sensed immediately that here was the fulfillment of that prophetic insight given to me in prayer, and with it came the vast com-

80

fort of knowing that our futures and hence our every
days are in God's hands. Had I not persisted in prayer,
I might too easily have said no to the new job and have
missed this realization of his providential care.

Let's examine how this matter of prayer-dialog inter-
locks with the discussion in Chapter 3 about the prin-
cipalities and powers that rage in our rifted universe.
In intercessory prayer both of these powers meet in
a uniquely new concept. Prayer for others (intercession) is a singularly Christian practice.

Prayer for someone else is not a ruse to trap God and
force his hand as if he doesn't want to do good for his
own. It isn't pummeling God to make him surrender to
our will. Of what value is intercessory prayer if I am not
personally acquainted with the person or institution for
which I am praying? Why is intercession one of the
ongoing ministries of Jesus on my behalf? Didn't he
cry, "It is finished!" on the cross?

I pondered all of these questions when Marge informed me of all the cards and letters that came assuring
me of intercession on my behalf. Just two weeks before
my accident I had been a speaker and involvement-
group leader for all the women who attended the national convention of the women of the American Lutheran Church. News of my accident sped across the
country as their national office sent word of it to key
district leaders. Thousands of them wrote of their prayer
support both as individuals and as groups, a vast sister-
hood of caring persons. Congregations we had served,
pastors from all denominations, friends in community
agencies, business people—all responded to my need in
the most loving demonstration of concern imaginable. A
young man in faraway Australia who had only been
present at one of our worship services wrote that he had

only recently had a personal encounter with Jesus, and that as he was praying for me, the Spirit made it clear to him that I would be healed.

I tried to sort out, as I lay there paralyzed, what all of this meant to me. I had always known that through intercessory prayer certain power is released. In specific instances, actual physical healings had taken place immediately and directly as a result of prayer. (But why not always?) I've seen a radical modification of people's thinking happen because of prayer projected on them. (But not always.) Lives have been transformed because caring others had pinpointed petitions for their spiritual wholeness. Didn't Ambrose say about Augustine, that the son of so many petitions could not go permanently lost?

What then is the mystery and possibility of intercessory prayer? The Word becomes flesh in whatever fashion we let it be born. We join battle against the psychic forces of evil insofar as we let the Spirit of Jesus control us. He releases his cosmic power and channels it through us to others. When I am part of his team for intercession, the levees of my selfishness are broken down and the healing waters of God's grace can flow through to others in need.

I know grace came to me in my need through the prayers of others.

One of the more dramatic demonstrations of the unusual power of intercessory prayer came through a pastor friend of ours by the name of Bill. For him, prayer for others takes the form of visualizations through which, as he prays, he sees mental pictures of the person's need and of the answer to that need. Then he prays according to the pictured need.

As he prayed for Erling, he "saw" him in three bibli-

cal situations. In the first one, he saw Jesus raising the daughter of Jairus from the dead (Luke 8:49 ff.), but as she sat up, Bill saw Erling take her place. In the second "picture" he saw Erling as Moses with his hands uplifted over the embattled Israelites. Whenever his hands grew weary and started to fall, the Israelite army started to lose the battle, so his brother Aaron and friend Hur had to support his arms (Exod. 17:12 ff.). In the third picture, Bill remembered the fall roundups which Erling's congregation celebrated at a park in North Hollywood. There he saw Erling dancing before the gathered parishioners just as King David danced in celebration of the return of the Ark of the Covenant to Jerusalem, "leaping and dancing before the Lord" (2 Sam. 6:16).

Bill called me two weeks after Erling's accident and asked to meet me at the church. There he told me about these remarkable visions of his friend's recovery. Indeed Erling had been literally raised from the dead; his arms, totally paralyzed, were being supported in beautiful fashion by all of his "friends" in the church so that his ministry in his congregation did not fail in any way; but, when Bill told me of his last vision of Erling dancing, I simply laughed! Erling had never danced in his life! Not only was this activity frowned upon in his home town church, but he was not naturally endowed with an aptitude for the dance.

But the fulfillment of this picture-prayer is one of the most delightful occurrences of Erling's hospitalization!

Three days before I was to leave the hospital, Joe informed me that he had planned an activity for me that would help him ascertain my level of neurological return.

Even though intercom music bathed the therapy center, Joe frequently hummed the tune, "Waltzing Matilda," under his breath. That day he gave me a pillow and said, "Hold it, pretend it's Matilda, and dance with her."

I tried to tell him that I had never danced before in my life. I tried it once, but the girl who attempted to teach me gave up in despair and suggested ice skating as a substitute. Joe laughed and proceeded to instruct me in the steps of the box waltz and a sort of "heel-toe-and-away-we-go" jig.

"Okay, start dancing to the music," Joe ordered.

With my right arm around the pillow and my useless left arm strapped across my chest, I began. Backwards, forwards, pirouette—movements that would have frightened me just a few stumbling days before. My daughter was sitting in the waiting room of the therapy unit and saw me come waltzing down the halls, unable to believe her eyes. I must have made a strange pastoral figure, dancing around with my hospital mini-gown revealing my skinny atrophied legs.

When Joe returned me to the therapy room, he told me to sit down and rest and went out to talk to Kristi. Later she told me that Joe had confided to her, "Your father really amazes me."

Kristi asked, "How come?"

Joe replied, "In all my years of working with patients in therapy, he's the first patient I've had with his kind of injury who reached the neurological plateau where he could dance."

When Joe wheeled me back to my room, without my talking to Kristi and hearing his comment to her, I said, "Isn't it amazing that a friend of mine had a vision of me about six weeks ago dancing like David before God."

Joe was visibly moved. In that moment we knew we were in the presence of One who does count the hairs of our heads and understands all of our needs, One who holds the years of our lives in the palm of his hand.

When you pray, you are invited into the secrets of God. Prayer tucks in his promises and personalizes them. In prayer God comes like a loving mother to surround us with love, to warm us with grace, and to bless us beyond description more than we ask or think.

My prayers for Erling bypassed petition for praise, and rarely did anxiety for him become coherent in either thought or word. There was so much to be thankful for!

How utterly fantastic 1) that we all happened to be at the beach the day of Erling's accident; 2) that the life guard just happened to be on the beach on a Thursday when normally no life guard was ever there during the week; 3) that Paul had just finished a first aid course and knew how to give mouth-to-mouth resuscitation; 4) that Kristi happened to be swimming right next to her father; 5) that the ambulance was free that moment; 6) that the emergency room which was normally rushed happened to be empty; 7) that the neurosurgeon who was normally not around in the afternoon happened to be close by. Or did all these things just happen?

"Above all that we ask or think. . . ." How true that was for us! I was so totally caught up in the wonder of his unmerited grace in our lives, that God should be so good to us when he didn't really have to be, that my every prayer was praise in the conviction that "in everything God works for good with those who love him, who are called according to his purpose" (Rom. 8:28).

What a marvel when we think of all the "coincidences" that happen when we live in the constant state of communication with God!

The neurosurgeon unknowingly defined prayer so well.

He met me in a small waiting room overlooking the ocean on an afternoon when Erling was down in physical therapy. I had not had an opportunity to speak with him about Erling's progress for three weeks since he had been on vacation.

"Is Erling making satisfactory progress?" I asked. He looked at me as though he had not heard right.

"Satisfactory progress? Mrs. Wold, do you realize that most people with your husband's type of injury never walk again? And here he is, walking unaided at six weeks!"

"When you say 'most people' do you mean 50%? 75%?" I asked.

Patiently, he answered again, "Most people with his kind of injury never walk again. It's the most crippling of all injuries. In fact not too many years ago, he wouldn't have lived at all."

"Then how do you account for his remarkable progress?" I asked, thinking of this amazing miracle and answer to prayer that was being performed in Erling's life. The doctor was thoughtful for a while. Then he gave an answer I shall not forget and which I wrote down as soon as he had left because it struck me as such a profound paraphrase of Romans 8:28, as quoted above:

"It would seem, Mrs. Wold, that the only explanation for your husband's remarkable progress lies in the fact that a most fortuitous combination of circumstances seems to have been operating most propitiously in his behalf." Hallelujah!

So I relearned in new dimensions the joy of praying for others. For the first time, and I say it to my shame, I joined in the fellowship of Jesus who prayed all night for others. The prayer life of the Bible is very personalized, as James says, "Pray for one another that you may be healed. The prayer of a righteous man has great power in its effects" (James 5:16).

During the night I lifted up before God virtual hosts of people. I started in one state, in one locale, and moved across the entirety of it, asking the Spirit to remind me of people I knew—officials, the sick, pastors, friends, faculty, an endless list. Through those weeks I moved in my spirit across all of America and then out beyond its confines to other segments of our world. The Spirit focused people on my mind whom I hadn't thought of— at least in prayer—for years. He seemed to pinpoint needs that I could lavish his love upon. I bathed folks with his mercy and blessed them with his love.

Among these prayed-for ones was a pastor in Los Angeles who lived many miles from my hospital and for whom I hadn't prayed for the longest time. One night I was with him in prayer for many hours. The very next morning, the only time that this had ever happened, he called me. At that time, I was physically unable to lift the telephone or even to reach for it, so a nurse came in and laid the instrument next to my ear. We were both stirred in the spirit, strangely aware that we were communing that day on the same wavelength before God.

It's fascinating when the whole world becomes one's prayer field. You are in his presence as you've never been before. The life in the Spirit becomes a phenomenon and a joy and a privilege beyond description. I could enter into the lives and livings of many and join with them in their battles to live the Christ-life. I know those who were lonely, depressed, overworked, pressured into corners. I knew professionals who had lost their personal touch. I knew some arrogant and pride-filled ones who were sealed off from the rest of life. I knew that all men and all women have the same needs in the psychic and the spiritual and the physical areas of life, and that the world is filled with one mass cry of pain.

I recalled a doctor telling that from 50-80% of all the patients in the hospital he served had a network of other than physical problems interlaced with their illness and sometimes creating it. All of us need others who will pray their way into our lives to carry part of the burden and to help us ascend to the throne room with his peace, promise, and security forever. Then even pain becomes a lilting, joyous, gladsome experience of the presence of God!

It's tragic if one never discovers the radiant privilege of being a constant petitioner before God until pressed by the hard edge of death.

Every day after Erling was released from ICU and the rules of his new location permitted me to visit him for seven hours each day, from one o'clock until eight o'clock in the evening, I watched Joe, the therapist, as he put Erling through the daily routine required to get his arms functioning again. Joe was never satisfied with repeating exercises just for the sake of repetition. Each day he pushed Erling to his ultimate limits for that day. Each day he had to realize a little more of his potential. Joe built progressively on everything that had been done before—feeling each muscle fiber, gauging its development, testing each joint and sinew, and starting each day's program with all the possibilities he knew were available.

I listened as he exhorted, cajoled, urged, motivated, and pushed Erling beyond the limit to which he had taken him the previous day. If the tight, stiff muscles did not hurt when he pushed them back, he knew he had to push them a little further. Even when Erling seemed to have reached his ultimate physical capacity for that moment—perspiration pouring from his head, breathing heavily, red-faced—Joe would say, "How come you're not pushing? Come on, Erling, you know when you've done all you can physically, then you've got to 'psych' yourself up to do a little bit more! Put at least 110% effort into it! Push! Harder! Harder! Come on, push!"

Every day was the same. Doing a little better than the day before was never enough for Joe. Yesterday's limits were for yesterday. Today's 110% had to push them back.

Joe permitted me to watch the therapy process so that I could appreciate what Erling had to go through to be restored to a functioning body. I, of course, could not help making some obvious reflections on the similarities between this daily physical workout and our spiritual exercises.

I wondered about my own Christian life and the fact that there are unlimited potentials available to me which I never explore. No doubt I'm not willing to pay the price, to take the necessary time, or to produce the 110% of effort required to push back the boundaries of spiritual perception a little bit more each day.

I don't like to think that it always takes breaking one's neck or having someone close to you break his neck, to force an examination of what all those potentials are.

I wondered, for instance, about the potential for having healing gifts. How often I had longed to know the secret of becoming a channel of God's healing power—for Stan and Jim and Josh and all the other sufferers in ICU. Jesus promised that his followers would heal as well as preach and teach. Is it because I'm not willing to pay the price, because I'm not willing to go through the agonizing effort of deep prayer communication to learn to know the mind of God that well? What keeps me from pushing back the limitations of my own spirit

89

*each day? Why am I content with a perception of God
that's so mundane and routine? Why is an academic perception of God all that we care to know?*

*Obviously, one of the prices we're not willing to pay
is this daily workout that someone in Erling's predicament must go through for the rest of his life, so that
part of every day is devoted to the same exercises, going
through the same steps, pulling the same weights,
stretching the same stretches. A great deal of disciplinary
effort is required for the whole process.*

*Maybe that's why we like to "cop out" when convicted
of the need for disciplined spiritual exercises by insist-
ing that we pray without ceasing. Which can all become
rather sloppy. Serendipity becomes our theme and "as
the Lord reminds me" our slogan. We're a soft people,
trained to live in the ease of affluence, available plumb-
ing, and the warm shower experience. Joe demonstrated
the need for the disciplined life required if we are ever
to push back the limits of experience into a new dimension of living.*

*The therapist's creed, "If you don't use it, you lose
it," was never enough for Joe. Hanging on was a negative
experience; the challenge was to grow.*

After I was moved from the closely supervised Intensive Care Unit with its hovering staff, I was faced with
the serious problem of how to summon a nurse when
I needed help at night. I was unable to operate the
device provided for this purpose because of my non-
functioning hands. I could neither reach the thing nor
push the button on it even if it were placed within reach.
During the day my roommates were kind enough to
call the nurse for me, but I did not want to waken them
during the night.

Finally I thought of a solution. Every room was con-

90

nected by an intercom to the nurses' station. Whenever a light appeared on their board they knew that the patient in that room had pressed the call button and they would respond over the intercom to ask the patient what was needed. I suggested that, since I was the only one with this communication problem, that the line be left open for me all through the night.

That solved it. The results were amazing. I simply whispered, "Wold, room 240," and my voice reached the nurse at the desk immediately.

Christians know an open line of communication with God the Father. He hears us, the Scriptures keep emphasizing, just as he always heard his Son, our Brother, when he prayed.

Prayer, then, is God . . . listening. Even a whisper from us is heard.

8 | to be lifted by hope

Driving west from Grand Forks, North Dakota, a few years ago, I found myself caught in an unexpected rainstorm. Without warning, the world around me became ominously gray and black. My speeding car was hurtling through the center of a churning vortex, a rotating tunnel of wind and rain so solid that I felt as if I were compressed by invisible forces.

The situation struck me as a vivid parable of human life, providing only movement, threat, danger, suffering, death. As I drove fearfully through this oppressive mid-afternoon gloom, I saw ahead of me the most brilliant of lights, intensified by the rain, slanting in from above as the end of the dark tunnel became visible to me.

Fear of the uncontrolled elements around me still gripped me, but now I recognized another dimension. I was in the light, as shafts of that distant brilliance thrust their way through the surrounding gloom and

92

bathed the road around me. Light was both my present destiny and my future destination.

Because of Jesus Christ, the brightness of hope lights up every present moment. Just as I saw those shafts of light in the thunderstorm, I now see hope streaming through three channels to make us see the ultimate concern of his love.

It's a light that first breaks in fullness through the *resurrection of our Lord.* St. Peter, stung by the memory of repeated excursions into the darkness, becomes totally captured by the light of a hope that finally controlled his spirit. "Blessed be the God and Father of our Lord Jesus Christ!" he exults. "By his great mercy we have been born anew to a living hope through the resurrection of Jesus Christ from the dead, and to an inheritance which is imperishable, undefiled, and unfading, kept in heaven for you" (1 Pet. 1:3-4).

Hope through the resurrection! Because my body had once functioned normally, I lived in hope knowing what complete healing could be. But that hope was only a distant reality. The hope for each day was part of the whole and accompanied by as much praise and celebration as any sudden, all-at-once miracle could ever be. The hope for each day was the slight movement of a finger, the lifting of a foot from the bed, the removal of a tube from the stomach, the ability to rotate a shoulder. We praised God for each reborn muscle, since each one became the down payment for a wholly restored body.

So through the light that bursts from the grave of his resurrection, the total Christ is made visible and available in the microcosmic resurrections of every day.

If the first channel through which hope pours is the resurrection, then the second must be the fact of our *reigning Lord.* The writer to the Hebrews was buoyed up by the fact that Christ's ascension gave a flaming hope to the people of God—fugitives, harassed, driven, without a permanent home. The author unveils the meaning of the ascension.

"Look," that anonymous prophet seems to say, "the Ascended One has plunged through the veil into the presence of God on our behalf, in order to drop an anchor into the very heart of God. This anchor holds. It's as steadfast as the promises of God. Grasp it. Hold on. Never let go. You can lose it, but if you grab it, you'll discover the amazing mystery that it has really grabbed you. And on the rim of the world stands Jesus forever mentioning you by name and wanting you to be his alone forever."

In the endurance contest of this life he wants us to emulate his own ministry. For Jesus knew a tragic time of anxiety, despair, constriction of spirit, but he hung on. He was a fugitive, too, and knew total abandonment by God and people. Still he does not scream against the darkness of despair; he does not try to shout down his sadistic tormentors. With him is absolute certainty that God is still around and still belongs to him even when he cries, "My God, my God, why have you forsaken me?"

God remains his chief passion. He recognizes his presence, and his heart is still focused on him. Even when hell moves in, he does not let go of his Father's hand. He earned his right to say, "In the world you shall have tribulation, but be of good cheer. I have overcome the world." He has broken his way through; he has become our release. Through him, as St. Paul dramatically reminds us, "the Father has delivered us from the dominion of darkness and transferred us into the kingdom of his beloved Son" (Col. 1:13).

The third ray of light which illuminates the darkness of

94

our current experience pours out of the promised *return of Jesus*. In the first chapter of Ephesians, Paul breaks into a rhapsody as he unveils layer upon layer of the glory that is attached to our hope. Peel off the cover of your eyes, he cries, for only then will you see the flaming hope to which he has called us, "the riches of his glorious inheritance in the saints" (Eph. 1:18). But the full passion of his anticipation is caught up in his pastoral comment to his brother Titus when his heart glows with the fact that we are "awaiting our blessed hope, the appearing of the glory of our great God and Savior Jesus Christ, who gave himself for us to redeem us" (Titus 2:13-14). For Paul all three glowing lights that flood from the great completed acts of Jesus: the resurrection, the reign, and the return—each one of these guarantees the other.

All my past experience of God's faithful love was the ground of hope for me. There had been other times of trial and suffering and always the experience had been one of victory in trouble.

Had I not called to him in the despair of adolescence when life's road seemed paved only with futility and meaninglessness? And hadn't he directed me to a freeway of salvation which transformed my life?

I could face the suffering resulting from Erling's accident with a confidence built on God's faithfulness in the past. Every time I had come to one of life's dead ends, God had opened a new and better way. The foundation of my hope was made out of the concrete experiences of a lifetime of proving God's lovingkindness.

All the previous knowledge of God's gracious working in our lives is deposited in our memories for recall at times like this. Often when I felt particularly helpless, unable to see Erling for more than those tiny ten-minute periods, I was sustained by one special grace-experience memory.

When Kristi was four years old, she had a particularly difficult tonsillectomy. Because of a tendency to hemorrhage she had to remain in the hospital an extra day and night. When the doctor released her, he warned us to call him or bring her back to the hospital if she started to bleed again.

When I got up to check her in the middle of that first night home, I noticed a tiny trickle of blood out of the corner of her mouth, leading to a widening brown stain on her pillow.

We were living in the country at that time, twelve miles away from the hospital. Our telephone was the kind you rang by hand to get the operator who ran the switchboard in her living room. Using the telephone after nine o'clock in the evening meant waking her.

I recall being very tired that night, having watched over Kristi in the hospital the night before. I felt unable to concentrate on the problem of what to do about her bleeding. To take her to the hospital meant waking our three other children, including an infant, and bringing them with us on the twelve-mile ride to the hospital.

I awakened Erling who carried Kristi downstairs to the living room and placed her, still asleep, on the couch. He then sat down in the old rocker, and I continued to stand in the archway separating the living room and the dining room in that country parsonage.

We were both too tired to pray aloud. In the heavy, anxious silence, I became aware of a clear white light in the room, which seemed to illuminate me in such a way that I felt transparent. Such a strange feeling, but not at all frightening. I asked Erling, "Did you feel that?"

He looked up in surprise and said, "Yes, did you?"

With shared wonder, we acknowledged that "the light" had brought an absolute sense of assurance to both of us that Kristi would be all right and that we need not worry.

So we simply carried her back upstairs, put her in her bed, and went back to sleep soundly ourselves. I think I would have doubted the whole experience if it had not been shared by both of us. And Kristi was definitely all right in the morning, without any evidence of additional bleeding. As I look back on that incident, I marvel at the boldness of our trust—putting her back in bed knowing that the trickle of blood was still there!

Apparently we were only able to do that because the presence of Jesus in the light experience was so real.

The similarity between that event and the light Erling saw in the water is remarkable. And the results in our lives were the same. How else could we have managed to live in such positive assurance of ultimate healing after Erling's accident? I certainly don't have that kind of strength in me by nature.

So experience of God's grace in the past produced hope in the present, and I could not only survive but I could actually celebrate his presence! "More than that, we rejoice in our sufferings, knowing that suffering produces endurance, and endurance produces character, and character produces hope, and hope does not disappoint us, because God's love has been poured into our hearts through the Holy Spirit which has been given to us" (Rom. 5:3-5).

And all the time the Spirit was bearing witness with my spirit that we were and are children of God, and hope never dimmed. It just kept saying "Amen" to the fact that God had never let us down! That was the basis for my hope, and in it I rejoiced.

Any type of hope has its redeeming qualities. Prisoners of war who came back from Vietnam reminded us that only the discipline of hope kept them from becoming victims of despair and ultimate death. At the core of their lives those who lived held on to a variety of hopes. For one it was a family who waited; for another, a fiancée; for another an idealization of the American Dream; for another, a fiercely glowing desire to stay alive. Each one stayed alive by the insistence of a hope that kept on infusing them with power to go on.

But there was always the nagging possibility for them that their hope was built on an illusion. The fiancée may have married someone else; the family may have dramatically changed in character; the American Dream may have become a part of their vanished past.

I saw the terrors of surrendered hope in the life of an old woman who shared some hours in physical therapy. Therapy always involves pain. The struggle with rebellious muscles is never easy. The old woman was recovering from hip surgery, and Joe the therapist knew that he could teach her to walk again. Every day for a week, I heard him patiently guiding her through the parallel bars of the walkway. Every day for a week she protested, saying that she just couldn't do it. From previous experience Joe knew that the light of hope was a reality for her, and he wanted her to catch a glimpse of what he saw.

For a while she tried to see that hope in terms of her faltering steps. But one day I saw the light go out for her. There was shattering pathos in the final closing of this chapter of her life. She simply said, "I quit," and sat down in her wheelchair.

Nothing Joe could say would change her mind. No promises, no threats, no pictures of other healings swayed her. It was so simply done and so terrifying final. That afternoon she went to a nursing home, never to walk again.

Without hope there is only death, even when one is medically alive.

Hope for the Christian becomes a servant word. I saw it mirrored in Jesus the Suffering Servant of God, who "knowing whence he came and where he was going" took a towel and washed his disciples' feet. Knowing both source and destination on the swaying, threatening bridge of time, he gave himself to total servanthood. When I see life through his eyes, hope becomes for me the galvanization of the fact that I can help define my own future.

I began to count the times comfort was given to me by others in the words, "This too will pass." While I appreciated the love and good intentions of the speaker, I rebelled against the despair of those words.

I didn't want the experience just to "pass." I wanted to drain from every moment all that it had to offer. Suffering, I was convinced, had meaning, and I was determined not to miss any of that meaning. If Paul's statement in Phil. 1:29 were true, and I had no reason to believe otherwise, then why should I not reach out and grip these words and sing Te Deums in my present situation? "For it has been granted to you that for the sake of Christ you should not only believe in him but also suffer for his sake."

Hope can be real only if the present has meaning, and the present has meaning only in the light of this hope.

I did not want to cheat the present of its meaning. I recalled the time I had back surgery, a spinal fusion. I knew God could heal me without the surgery if he so willed, but I was positive in my conviction that I must go to the hospital. One of my roommates was a 24-year-

old mother of two. She had inoperable cancer of the brain. We became friends, and through my contacts with her some of the women in our church also befriended her, and in the six month period before she returned to the hospital to die, they served her physical and spiritual needs. As a result she one day asked me that great question, "Marge, what do I have to do to become a Christian?"

I thought of Lydia, the Bible teacher in Fort Worth, Texas, who was murdered one dark night coming home from her post office job. We all cried, "Why, God?" Four months later, Lydia's killer was hanged on the gallows at Huntsville, but before he died he confessed that he had been brought to Christ in prison and went to his death singing hymns of praise.

If suffering in some way serves the cause of Christ, then I wanted to be fully aware of what was going on. I wanted no part of any despairing passage of time; I wanted the tingling anticipation of hope working out its meaning in my life every minute.

A Christian is captured by a whole new dimension. Hope provides a new vibrancy and an aliveness. The world becomes God's place of business where he asks us to get his things done. A person lives only in the number of places where he touches life. The everyday becomes a glad "service center" where one looks for opportunities to be a servant of the One who is our only "hope of glory." Miracles become everyday. One is charged with the anticipation that fantastic things can happen to *me* right now.

Since my accident I live anticipating. Jesus never lets anyone down. Life gets so exciting at times that I feel like bursting with praise and adoration. I think of someone that I ought to see, for instance, and the moment

100

the thought prayerfully touches my mind, that person calls. A problem thwarts me when I've gone through a growing bit of agony, and the answer comes before I've made any effort to find it.

My hope grows because of a gift-giving God who beggars any attempt at praise and service. It becomes fascinating to be a Christian because hope makes a transparency of life and we discover again that if we "walk in the light [of hope] as he is in the light, we have fellowship with one another, and the blood of Jesus Christ his son keeps cleansing us from all our sin."

Therefore I keep asking myself, am I plunging down all the avenues of service that he makes available for the expression of this hope? Do I help the hurt, the hungry, the broken, the bitter, the defeated, the despairing, that in the hope offered by Christ there are new options for today and tomorrow? Do I fight to make life more palatable and joyous for every neighbor?

I was sitting some months after my injury by the window in our home. I was haunted by the thought that my body seemed to be so slow in recovering. Having never been sick before, I found it hard to adjust to what seemed to be a slow process toward wholeness. The sun was streaming in over my right shoulder. I was reading the prophets when all of a sudden from Jeremiah 29 a verse broke me open with hope renewed that fills me still: "For I know the plans I have for you, says the Lord. They are plans for good and not for evil, *to give you a future and a hope*" (v. 11). I called my wife at her office to share this with her. It became the channel of another hope-light. It revolutionized my spirit. The future is God's. *Shadows* are not his "thing;" *light* is! Hope is his specialty and he offers himself again, "Christ in you, our hope of glory."

The light of hope that floods the soul of the New Testament comes from realities fulfilled and anticipated. The light of hope breaks out from the resurrection tomb; it's let loose with a present vitality by the fact of a reigning Christ; it's captured in a new dimension in the basic Bible fact that Jesus Christ will "come again."

This is the matrix from which miracles are born.

9 | to come alive as a witness

Early on a bright Sunday morning just one month after I was brought to the hospital, three nurses walked into my room and announced that I needed a new bed. Apparently there was some malfunction in the electric device that raised and lowered my bed that made it impossible for them to give me my morning bath.

"You've been up in a wheelchair, haven't you?" asked a new nurse whom I'd never seen before.

"Until now, only the physical therapist has been permitted to get him out of bed, and he isn't here on weekends," answered one of the nursing assistants.

The decision was made that I could safely be helped out of bed and tied into the wheelchair with bedsheets. Then my bed could be switched with a new one while I was out of the room.

"We'll get Bill to help us, and we'll put you out in the visitor's alcove where you can look out over the ocean for a while," the nurse informed me.

103

They left to get Bill, the male nurse, and I went back to my morning reverie. Through most of that night I had been in joyous prayer. My special focus had been my wife. That morning she was to give the first of two Sunday sermons in our congregation. My spirit was persuaded that this morning was to be crucial in the life of our parish, and it was our first personal communication with them since my accident. As I lifted Marge before God's throne, total peace came to me and at 8:15 that morning I knew without a shadow of a doubt that a real breakthrough of the Spirit was to be a product of our joint sermonic communication that morning.

I was free at that moment to concentrate on my own ministry in the hospital.

"God," I prayed, "I am your servant. For 30 years I've been used to preaching on Sunday mornings. Right now I can't do that, but I'm still your witness. What do you want me to do this morning?"

The nurses returned with Bill, the wheelchair, and a stack of linen. Bill, the strong man, helped lift me out of bed and I was soon strapped into my rolling cocoon and being wheeled down the hall toward the alcove that looked down on the coast highway and the shimmering waters of the Pacific.

At the last moment the nurse changed her mind about going there.

"If I put you in that room, there won't be anyone to watch you," she said, thinking aloud. "I'd better put you out here in the hall near the nurses' station so someone can keep an eye on you."

With that decision made, she parked me outside the closed door of a corner room, set the brake on the wheelchair and left.

I sat there, the neck brace which I wore day and night holding me stiffly erect, my body tightly bound in the

104

chair, my useless arms propped up on two pillows in my lap, and waited. I tired easily and kept wishing they would hurry and get my bed ready.

The door of the corner room opened. A tiny woman, lovely with a fragile, doll-like beauty, came out of the room, smiled at me and went to the nurses' station. She returned to the room, and a little later the door opened again and once more she made her way to the nurses' desk, spent a brief time in conversation with the ward clerk and returned to the room.

The third time the door opened, she stopped in front of my wheelchair.

"You're Pastor Wold, aren't you?"

There was nothing to do but admit that this was the case so I said, "Yes."

"I know who you are because we have the same night nurse, and she's told us all about you," she said, her beautiful eyes probing my face.

Then I knew who the owner of that tender countenance was. My Catholic night nurse, one of the most sensitive persons on the hospital staff, had told me about the man who lay in the corner room slowly dying of Parkinson's disease, heart failure, and the aftereffects of throat surgery. He had been there three months, and his wife lived in the room with him to be near him and to devote herself wholly to his care.

The lovely woman was the wife of the dying cowboy actor, a man who was a legend from the early days of television, the white-haired champion of justice who rode the plains of the TV screen on a white horse. For thirty-eight years they had been married, inseparable in their devotion, childless. Members of the staff had communicated to me their concern for her because of the intensity of her love for her husband and their fear that she might break down totally when he died.

I knew again that God had set the scene, as he always does when our desire is to be used by him. Overwhelmed by the knowledge that God had arranged this moment for me, my heart exulted: Use me, Lord, let me speak your word.

Then it was that she asked me to tell her about my experience and what it had meant to me. For 22 minutes I poured out the glories that I had experienced with Jesus Christ. Her eyes, reflectors of the soul, never left my face. I had not known a more intrigued listener. Tears welled up as Jesus' spirit made it clear to her that she was one of his. I could plead with her because she had opened her heart to me, and I didn't stop until I was totally exhausted.

As though responding to some divine cue, at that precise moment her business manager came to call her aside, and my nurse came to push me to the alcove where I was originally destined to go so that I could view the ocean for a few moments before going to my new bed. Never had the waters appeared lovelier!

I never saw the cowboy star's wife again and two days later he died. The nurses told me that she left the hospital with courage and peace.

My hospital stay was an ideal time for me to be a witness, to talk about my experience with Jesus whenever the opportunity came. My physical needs were being cared for by others, and I had no other responsibilities. All the time I had could be devoted to my witness of the resurrection.

Witnessing is a comprehensive term. In our vocabulary it has never been limited to words alone. In fact, if Erling had been an impossibly demanding and fussy patient, I, along with all the other patients in the hospital (to say

nothing of the staff members!) would probably have writ-
ten off his "witness" as a big zero!

Didn't Martin Luther say something to the effect that
being a Christian is not what one believes about such
matters as the Virgin Birth but how one treats a servant
in the home?

The test of the genuineness of our Christian witness
comes when we are under pressure, rubbed raw by the
machinery of living. The secret is not to concentrate on
our own performance but to be lost in the needs of
others. Erling forgot about his own situation in his con-
cern for those around him who had needs similar to his
but lacked the faith to match their needs. His one desire
was to share his faith with them.

If we ever let ourselves become God's devotees, he
floods our lives with possibilities for witnessing. I had a
number of roommates, none of them Christians. I had
endless hours with all of them in which to discuss their
relationship with God and to share my relationship with
Christ. Staff members would come, as well as patients. All
of them had needs.

When I was finally able to be in the wheelchair at night
after visiting hours were over, I propelled myself around
with my feet looking for those who needed a friend. My
own physical distress made me a brother to others who
knew physical disability. This very fact made God's words
penetrate much skepticism and despair. For once I really
felt totally consumed by witnessing, and I understood the
passion expressed by a famous young black singer, who
said, "Rock gets in my whole body, my whole soul. It
knocks me out. I kills me. If I couldn't do that, *I wouldn't
be.*" Substitute the word "witnessing" for "rock" and you
get the message.

107

What's needed for all of us is a personal experience with Jesus Christ. The words of Boris Pasternak whose heart's blood was poured out in the novel *Doctor Zhivago* keep coming back to me. Sensing man's insanity to man brought him great personal suffering. As a Jew in Russia his personal pain was only augmented. Ever since his death, I recall those burning words of his in which he summarized his own spiritual experience: "I could not have endured it without my discovery of Jesus Christ. *He came to me!*" That, to me, is the secret of witnessing.

Other gifts and talents may help, but they are only peripheral to this fact, "Jesus came to me!"

All that we are becomes our agenda. Witnessing never stands apart from this fact. I do not set aside certain hours for witnessing. I do not plan a "program" of witnessing. I witness. Constantly. By all that I am. And by all that I am not.

Above all, I am human. To try to pretend that my witness stands apart from my humanity is an impossible assumption to live up to. I am human, therefore I will sometimes do all that human beings tend to do. I will get angry, occasionally indulge in pouting and self-pity, and probably most of the time forget that I'm witnessing all of the time!

Witnessing then is agenda-less. But it is never insensitive or unaware. And it is always honest and unmasked. It can repent and it can forgive. That's probably the most effective witnessing.

Witnessing is ministry. Verbalization of one's relationship with Jesus is essential. "He that confesses me before men, him will I confess before my Father in heaven," Jesus said. Nevertheless, the realism of the life of Jesus is attached first to what he *did* and then to what he *said*.

Luke tells us, "I have dealt with all that Jesus began to do and teach" (Acts 1:1).

Jesus lived his message before he spoke it. More than that, he only *began* his ministry and left its continuation for you and me. When he stood as a witness in the Capernaum synagogue, he outlined the total ministry for everyone who wants to follow him. His reading was incisive and clear from the prophet Isaiah. "The Spirit of the Lord is upon me, because he has anointed me to preach good news to the poor. He has sent me to proclaim release to the captives and recovering of sight to the blind, to set at liberty those who are oppressed, to proclaim the acceptable year of the Lord" (Luke 4:18-19).

Vivid in memory is the statue of Christ I saw at the end of a hospital corridor. It was a replica of Thorvaldsen's Christ, hands outstretched over one more institution where the needs of people are particularized. On the base of the statue I saw the Latin phrase, *Caritas Christi urget me.* (The love of Christ compels me.)

The love of Christ compels me to try to get at the source of the wretched boredom that is a funeral pall over so much of the world: the anger of the oppressed, of the dispossessed and the forgotten poor; the emptiness in lives that keep people from any meaningful relationship. To be a witness is to be a reflector of Christ on every level of life.

So I ask myself, "Why was I sent back? Why didn't the Lord let me die?"

Almost everyone I met in the hospital was searching for some sure word about his or her own end. My own dedicated neurosurgeon was searching for an answer to life and death and really wanted to know. The brilliant computer specialist who roomed with me and who, though only 47, had suffered several heart attacks, wanted to know the ultimate answer to life more than anything else.

109

So few had found the answer. No human formula is ever sufficient. It is as Dr. Basile Yanovsky of the New York City venereal disease clinic says when he sees a part of the 2.5 million Americans who contract VD annually: "I get the . . . impression . . . from all these singles, couples, and triangles, young and old, hetero- and homosexuals, these wives, husbands, lovers, and mistresses [that] they are after something else, and sex is only a substitute, which, apparently, does not satisfy them. . . . Every time I stick in my needle I feel: penicillin is not enough!" Whether it be through sex, work, religion, recreation, or some other avenue, everyone is on a search for meaning.

I believe I was sent back to give this one man's witness to the meaning of life and death. *I* found God faithful in trouble; *I* found Jesus real; *I* tasted the resurrection glory; *I* found ecstasy in suffering; *I* found a supportive fellowship in family and friends; I found that *for me* Jesus is life and hope!

This is my testimony.

epilog

On the morning of Erling's surgery, a violent summer storm erupted. Storms are rare in southern California, and in August rain of any kind is unusual. On that Saturday just two days after Erling's accident, winds of hurricane force whipped the coastline into snarling fury.

I sat alone in the sheltering quiet of the hospital corridor waiting for Erling to be wheeled from Intensive Care to surgery when without warning all the lights went out. Only the glowing exit signs relieved the darkness. Immediately my thoughts went to those patients, my husband included, who were dependent on electrically powered machinery for the maintenance of their vital functions—heart monitors, stomach pumps, respirators, dialysis units.

Before I had time to really explore the full implication of this loss of power for Erling's impending surgery and for all those other lives, the lights flickered once, came on at half their power, and then flared brightly once more.

111

Later I learned that when the storm disrupted the normal flow of power, the hospital's own generators began functioning, and this alternate, emergency source of energy took over almost immediately.

In much the same way, I think Erling and I were operating on an alternate source of power after the accident, power which is always available but too often reserved only for the stormy days of our lives.

I'm still dependent on that other source of power for strength to face the life that is now mine. The support machinery is no longer needed, the neck brace now lies unused in a dresser drawer, and I am trying to take up my ministry again. Even so, every day is a struggle with unwilling muscles and a coping with new and disturbing body sensations.

So as soon as we had come to the end of this book, I realized that this account of my ocean encounter and subsequent experience of God's grace and power is only the beginning of the story that must be told.

The rest of it must deal with these days when grace still provides the only power that makes it possible to live with, and to triumph over, despair.

My disabilities sometimes assume the proportions of a mountain whose torturous slopes must be conquered daily. On each side of my rocky path yawns a dark abyss of frustration and despair.

In spite of this, I am learning that I can still praise God and mean it when I say, "Hey God, thanks for the mountain!" But that's the rest of my story—a story I live out as I climb my mountain, discovering on its lonely heights the presence and power of God.